The
I Found It!
Series

POWER AND PRAYERS TO PREVAIL OVER SPIRITUAL GARMENTS OF HINDRANCE

REVERSING CURSES THAT DISTORT IDENTITY IN THE SPIRITUAL REALM

JOSHUA TAYO OBI-GBESAN

PRESS

To the Good Shepherd who divested me of a garment of hindrance and chose me to proclaim liberty to other captives

Acknowledgments

First and foremost, I give glory and honor to the Lord who empowered me, by the Holy Spirit, to compile this handbook.

Unending thanks to my lovely wife, Marion B. Obigbesan, for her support, perseverance, and ceaseless words of encouragement...

My sincere appreciation for the prayer support and backing of Apostle Samuel A. Sotade and the ministers and members of Mountain of Fire and Miracles Ministries (Colorado, U.S. Branch)...

My special thanks also to Donna Scuderi, who was divinely connected to undertake the rigors of editing and correcting the manuscript...

And grateful acknowledgment to my father in the Lord, the dynamic General Overseer of the Mountain of Fire and Miracles Ministries worldwide, Dr. Daniel K. Olukoya, whose boundless gift of writing has influenced my writing of this book.

Contents

Introduction

Your Spiritual "Wardrobe"

Every day in our natural lives, we choose which clothing we will wear and to whom we will present ourselves in the attire chosen. The decision is a significant one; the garments we select affect the way we feel about ourselves and the responses we receive from others. This is true at home, in the workplace, and in other settings. The manner of our dress *matters*.

The same is true in the spirit realm. Each of us is clothed— whether unwittingly or by choice—in spiritual "garments." This unseen wardrobe affects our outcomes: it influences both our conduct and outlook and it determines which spiritual entities will be "attracted" to us. Clearly, the spiritual garments we wear play a critical role in our life outcomes.

All too often, however, we are keenly aware of the *ways* in which our lives are playing out, but completely in the dark as to *why*. We fail to realize the forces at work in the invisible, spiritual world. We are oblivious to the fact that our habitual ways of living determine the nature of our spiritual garments (and vice versa) and, therefore, the connection between our life experiences and the clothing of the unseen realm.

Do you know someone whose habitual ways of living seem bent toward evil? These tendencies are not happenstance: an individual who traffics in evil is clothed in some form of it, spiritually speaking. Likewise, those whose habitual life conduct is good, pure, and holy, are clothed in corresponding spiritual garments.

The spiritual garments we wear always match our real-life character—the nitty-gritty version of us that lives behind the facades. Dr. Daniel Olukoya, General Overseer of the Mountain of Fire and Miracles Ministries worldwide, says it this way: "Your spiritual garments determine your spiritual position."

Everyone born into this world enters life wearing an invisible spiritual garment. The type of spiritual garment is not chosen by the newborn. Instead, the child's spiritual garments (and therefore spiritual position) are determined by the kinds of lives lived by the child's parents and other ancestors. Whether the spiritual garments are divine or touched by evil, the child bears the spiritual "marks" of those who have gone before.

Because we are all the offspring of Adam and Eve, every one of us was born wearing garments of sin. None of us entered this world undefiled. All of us bore the stain of sin initiated in the Garden of Eden; each of us took our first breath under the weight of transgression and in dire need of salvation.

While all of us were born into sin, some of us experienced more exposure to demonic powers than others. This exposure begins in the womb. Mothers who dabble in the demonic (by taking evil concoctions or having contact with demonic agents, for example) can cause their unborn children to be invested with evil spiritual garments. Although these children are innocent of evil pursuits, they will contend with the forces of darkness from the day they are born.

Unless the matter is spiritually discerned and addressed, the battle can continue for a lifetime. Yet, that needn't be the case! Jesus' death and resurrection have given every human being the opportunity to shed the defiled garments of sin and be clothed in the undefiled garments of salvation! Praise the Lord!

As in the Natural, So in the Spiritual

David expressed the condition of every newborn when he said, *"Behold, I was shapen in iniquity; and in sin did my mother conceive me"* (Ps. 51:5). He understood the circumstances and implications of his birth and looked to God for restoration.

The death and resurrection of Christ were planned by God to provide this restoration. The Savior made it possible for a sin-scarred man or woman to be raised up to righteousness and eternal life. This required a transformation, one which the apostle Paul witnessed by revelation. Paul was shown the distinctions between the natural body and the spiritual one. In First Corinthians 15:44 he wrote, under the inspiration of the Holy Spirit:

[In physical death, the human body] *is sown a natural body; it is raised a spiritual body. There is a natural body, and there is a spiritual body.*

We cover our natural bodies with physical clothing. The clothes we choose to wear can attract others to us or repel them from us. The condition of our spiritual clothing likewise brings either acceptance or rejection. Just as our physical garments can smell sweet or acrid; our spiritual garments can carry an odor that is pleasant or off-putting. The very scent of our clothing can entreat acceptance and harmonious relationships or incite rejection, abandonment, and even hatred.

In the physical realm, the clothing we wear can affect our moods:

All thy garments smell of myrrh, and aloes, and cassia, out of the ivory palaces, whereby they have made thee glad (Ps. 45:8).

When we are well-dressed and carefully groomed, we are in better spirits. When our spiritual clothing is in good order, it has the parallel effect, but on a spiritual level.

Whether in the natural or the spiritual realm, clothing can become worn. Even the finest garments can become frayed or fall into disarray. Naturally speaking, our clothing can become defiled through personal carelessness, insufficient laundering, or physical attacks against the wearer. Spiritual garments can be defiled by sin and begin to work against us, by dint of their poor condition.

These garments of hindrance constrict our progress and limit our ability to fulfill our God-given callings. They adversely affect our marriages, relationships, advancement, businesses, careers, academics, and so on. Such garments attract "matching" outcomes. This is the reason for many of our struggles in life: unfavorable events and results follow those who wear such clothing; the very blessings of God are repelled by them.

Glorious spiritual garments are available! Undefiled spiritual garments, or garments of blessing, are the divine garments we were created to wear. Any believer who puts on these divine garments will experience victory in the battle against the adversary and see evil flee from them. They will enter the Kingdom of heaven having run the course and completed the race to the glory of God (see 2 Tim. 4:7).

The Bible says *"My people are destroyed for lack of knowledge..."* (Hosea 4:6). Conversely, the people of God can flourish when knowledge is found and applied in faith to the course of their lives.

We are about to discover, on the basis of Scripture, which spiritual garments we are wearing, which ones we need to remove, and which ones we ought to put on. This spiritual act will transform not only our spiritual lives, but our experiences in the natural world.

May God bless you abundantly as you journey with me in this worthy endeavor!

Chapter 1

A Change of Clothes

Many years ago, I had a dream which revealed to me the manner and degree to which the spirit realm controls the physical realm. The dream demonstrated clearly the role of our spiritual garments in shaping our natural, physical lives.

In the dream, I wore stained clothing. As I walked down the street in my unsightly attire, another poorly-dressed man walking in the opposite direction tried to engage me in a fight. As I prepared to defend myself, a third man—an old man—appeared from nowhere, took my hand, and led me into a house. Once inside the house, my dirty clothes were stripped from me, and a new set of clothes (including new shoes) was given me. As the old man led me back onto the street, I awoke from the dream.

I had this dream during a short nap following an all-night prayer meeting. When I awoke, I had a revelation: I realized that, if what I saw in the dream was indicative of my spiritual state, there was no way anything good could come to me or around me. My physical living conditions certainly bore out this revelation: at that time my situation was dire. I was poor and lonely, with no help in sight. I knew I was in need of His help, and I thanked the Lord for coming to deliver me!

This dream signified the beginning of my deliverance. The "change of clothes" that I received in the dream began to produce manifestations in the physical realm. Here is my testimony of the transformation that occurred:

A few days after my dream, I travelled back to my business base. Everything around me had changed. People who never saw anything of value in me began to give me gifts. Those from whom I never expected help began to offer their assistance. The change caused the people closest to me to wonder what was happening. It was simple: the God of wonders had visited me and changed my spiritual garments!

There is another piece of this testimony that I must share: On the night that I returned to my business base, I went to see a friend who was in the military at the time. A friend of his who happened to be a car dealer was there visiting. When the visit between them was over, the dealer went on his way.

As he returned to his car, he saw my aging vehicle parked near his. He came back into the house to ask who owned the old car. I told him I did. He asked me to bring my old car to his stall and exchange it for the new car of my choice. He said I could arrange to pay the balance later by whatever payment mode I found suitable!

This unusual offer was no coincidence. My garments of hindrance had been removed and new garments of honor and blessing had been invested in me. My life changed for the better from that point forward.

The Origin of Spiritual Garments

In those days, I had no idea how I came to wear defiled spiritual garments. Whether they were self-imposed, inherited, or invested in me through some form of witchcraft, I did not know.

Later, through self-examination, research of my ancestral lineages, and much prayer, I began to understand the process that led to my being hindered in the spirit realm. Having also learned more about the ministry of deliverance over the years, I decided to put my findings in writing for the benefit of others.

You are among those for whom this book was written. But before we continue, please pause for a moment and pray this prayer, inviting God to lead your quest for revelation:

O God of wonders, visit me in Your mercy and remove the garments of hindrance that have been forcefully put on me by contrary powers, in the name of Jesus.

"Garment" Essentials

In the most fundamental sense, a garment is a covering. A garment can be any article of clothing; but for our purposes, it is especially any type of clothing (a coat or dress, for example) that is worn over the undergarments.

As already mentioned, we wear both physical and spiritual garments. Let's consider our physical garments first, as they provide insights that also apply to the garments we wear in the spirit realm.

The first thing we notice about someone's attire is the effect upon the person's appearance and the impression it conveys to us about the person's being. Physical garments tell us a great deal about:

1. **The personality of the individual.** The type of clothing being worn tells us about nature of the person wearing it. Certain attire is worn by royalty. Those in the military wear garments that are distinct from those civilians wear. Some garments are worn by males; others are worn by females and clearly indicate femininity. In other words, an article of clothing can tell a very specific story about the wearer's life.

2. **The wealth of the individual.** A person's wardrobe gives us clues as the individual's financial status. It is often easy to tell whether the individual is wealthy or poor, simply by the choice of garments being worn.

3. **The tribe of the individual.** Clothing can provide distinct cultural, ethnic, and geographical clues. Often, clothing can speak specifically to a person's tribal origin.

4. **The profession or career of the individual.** Based on one's garments, we can often determine what kind of work the person does. A soldier's clothing (including helmet, camouflage, boots, etc.) is different from a doctor's attire (surgical scrubs or a white coat and stethoscope).

5. **The state of mind of the individual.** Often, the garments worn by an individual can provide clues as to the state of their mental health (as in the case of the untreated, uncared for, mentally ill individual who is left wearing the same soiled clothes for weeks).

6. **The mood of individual:** Certain garments indicate a state of mourning (dark colors, veils, etc.), while other clothing suggests a celebratory mood (such as bright colors and patterns, bridal wear, etc.).

Physical attire reveals many internal and external facets of an individual's life. Spiritual garments also reveal a great deal, including elements of the wearer's spiritual history and aspects of his or her physical state.

Spiritual attire tells the story of what is going on in the person's life at a given moment in time. As we learn more about spiritual garments, we will come to understand what those garments produce and precisely what story they tell.

Chapter 2

How Spiritual Garments Are Invested

Investment Through Habitual Living

As we know, physical and spiritual garments can reveal a great deal about an individual's identity: physical garments are seen and assessed by physical eyes; spiritual garments are perceived and assessed by spiritual eyes.

The way we choose to live in the physical realm affects us spiritually; our ongoing choices and actions generate the spiritual garments with which we will become clothed. For example, a person who chooses a life of habitual sin will be invested with particular types of spiritual garments of hindrance. Conversely, one who chooses to live in righteousness will be invested with particular types of divine garments.

Spiritual garments are revealed when our spiritual eyes are opened by the Lord, whether through dreams or any other means of revelation. One Biblical example of the revelation of spiritual knowledge and truth was experienced by the prophet Zechariah:

And he shewed me Joshua the high priest standing before the angel of the LORD, and Satan standing at his right hand to resist him. And the LORD said unto Satan, The LORD rebuke thee, O Satan; even the LORD that hath chosen Jerusalem rebuke thee: is not this a brand plucked out of the fire? (Zech. 3:1-2).

Zechariah had a vision in which the Lord showed him Joshua the high priest standing before the angel of the Lord. Joshua had been performing his priestly duties when Satan appeared and resisted him. Satan attempted to obstruct the spiritual right of Joshua the high priest to perform his duties before the Lord. Almighty God, who watches over the affairs of men, personally intervened and rebuked Satan.

The reason for Satan's attempt to hinder Joshua was not revealed until the next verse:

*Now Joshua was **clothed with filthy garments**, and stood before the angel* (Zech. 3:3, emphasis added).

This verse clearly shows the spiritual state of Joshua the high priest as he stood before Christ (the Angel of the Lord). He was wearing what the Bible calls *filthy garments*. In other words, Joshua was invested with specific garments of hindrance referred to as *filthy garments*. These gave Satan the legal ground to resist him in his priestly assignments.

Now the question is, how did Joshua the high priest come to be dressed in filthy garments? Who put the filthy garments on him? And, was he aware of the filthy garments he was wearing? Zechariah 3:4 provides important insight:

And he answered and spake unto those that stood before him, saying, Take away the filthy garments from him. And unto him he said, Behold, I have caused thine iniquity to pass from thee, and I will clothe thee with change of raiment.

Although he was a high priest, Joshua was declared to be a man of iniquity. Whether he did so consciously or unconsciously, he had lived a life of habitual sin. As a result, Joshua the high priest was clothed in filthy garments.

According to this vision, I believe that Christ (before whom Joshua the high priest was standing) instructed the angelic beings to remove the filthy garments from Joshua precisely at the moment he was granted forgiveness for his sins. The Bible does not say what kind of sin Joshua committed. Yet we see clearly that sin was the issue, because the Lord said *"I have caused thine iniquity to pass from thee"* (Zech. 3:4).

Sin was the means by which Joshua became clothed with filthy garments. Therefore the Lord ordered Joshua to be divested of them. However, the Lord did not stop there; He also promised to replace the filthy garment with a *"change of raiment* [clothing]."

Zechariah 3:5 shows that Joshua the high priest was clothed by God in new spiritual garments that Satan could not come against. These were the garments of the high priest as prescribed in Exodus 28:4. Among them was a mitre, to cover the high priest's head:

And I said, Let them set a fair mitre upon his head. So they set a fair mitre upon his head, and clothed him with garments. And the angel of the Lord stood by (Zech. 3:5).

The high priestly garments were holy garments for glory and for beauty! They were the garments he was ordained to wear.

The story of Joshua the high priest is relevant to us today. The above passage of Scripture yields the following five spiritual revelations:

1. Habitual sinful living in the everyday life of Joshua translated into a wardrobe of filthy garments of hindrance.
2. These garments of hindrance gave Satan legal ground from which to hinder the high priest from performing his duties before the Lord.
3. The forgiveness of sin makes way for the removal of filthy spiritual garments.

4. Satan's resistance to Joshua would end when the garments were changed.

5. Even after the Lord rebuked Satan, the legal ground for Satan's resistance had to be removed. Joshua's sins were forgiven him and his filthy spiritual garments were changed to priestly garments that neither Satan nor any of his agents could come against.

Many people today are living their lives in such a way as to produce a spiritual wardrobe that gives legal ground for attack to the forces of darkness. As they carry on their lives in "filthy" spiritual attire, they are continually hindered by the enemy and often unaware of the cause.

It is a simple equation: we are spirit beings, first and foremost. Therefore, we will always be clothed, spiritually speaking. More specifically, we will be adorned with spiritual garments that match our habitual modes of living. If those garments are unholy, our physical lives will reflect that.

Had Joshua the high priest remained in his iniquity, without forgiveness and without a "change of clothes," he would have continued to experience hindrances in his ministerial duties. Absent forgiveness and redemption, the sequence of habitual living and the creation of spiritual garments operates along two self-perpetuating tracks:

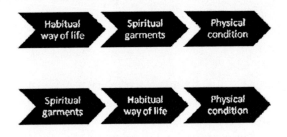

Habitual ways of living generate matching spiritual garments which, in turn, bring about physical situations that correspond to the types of spiritual garments being worn. A change in one's way of life, a cry to the Lord for help, or even an unsolicited act of divine intervention (as in the case of Joshua the high priest), can strip away evil spiritual garments so that the physical life improves and, in turn, affects the cycle in a positive way. Regardless of the manner of deliverance, the source of contrary spiritual garments must be dealt with in order for the desired outcomes to be realized.

Investment by Inheritance

The Bible shows clearly that undefiled spiritual garments can be inherited. So it is with evil spiritual garments.

And the holy garments of Aaron shall be his sons' after him, to be anointed therein, and to be consecrated in them. And that son that is priest in his stead shall put them on seven days, when he cometh into the tabernacle of the congregation to minister in the holy place (Exod. 29:29-30).

A male child born in the lineage of Aaron inherited his garments of priesthood. As a nation, the children of Israel inherited garments of blessing from Abraham, whom God blessed (see Gen. 12:2-3). On the other hand, Dathan and Abiram of the tribe of Reuben inherited evil spiritual garments that issued from the curse declared on Reuben by Jacob (see Gen. 49:4). They failed to excel, just as the curse dictated, and instead rebelled against Moses and suffered the consequences (see Num. 16).

Not even Moses escaped the consequences of a sin-based inheritance. The great force of anger inherited from his great grandfather, Levi (see Gen. 49:5-7) invested him with garments of hindrance. His anger manifested when he murdered an Egyptian (see Exod. 2:12); when he smashed the tablets of the Ten Commandments to the ground (Exod. 32:19); and when he struck the rock twice, instead of speaking to it as God commanded (Num. 20:11). As a result, Moses did not make it into the Promised Land.

Investment by Transfer

In Isaiah 22, the Lord sent the prophet Isaiah to Shebna, the secretary of King Hezekiah. Isaiah told Shebna that, because of his pride, he would be stripped of the robe (garment) of honor. Isaiah foretold that Shebna's robe would be transferred to Eliakim the son of Hilkiah:

> *And it shall come to pass in that day, that I will call my servant Eliakim the son of Hilkiah: and I will clothe him with thy robe, and strengthen him with thy girdle, and I will commit thy government into his hand: and he shall be a father to the inhabitants of Jerusalem, and to the house of Judah* (Isa. 22:20-21).

This transfer occurred in both the natural and spiritual realms. Eliakim received the robe of honor by divine pronouncement. This spiritual act resulted in specific spiritual and physical outcomes:

> *And the key of the house of David will I lay upon his shoulder; so he shall open, and none shall shut; and he shall shut, and none shall open. And I will fasten him as a nail in a sure place; and he shall be for a glorious throne to his father's house. And they shall hang upon him all the glory of his father's house, the offspring and the issue, all vessels of small quantity, from the vessels of cups, even to all the vessels of flagons* (Isa. 22:22-24).

Just as the Lord transferred the goodly robe from Shebna to Eliakim, Satan and his agents transfer evil garments of shame from one person to another. However, those covered with the blood of Jesus can only be affected by these transfers if they make themselves vulnerable, through sin, to Satan's advances. In so doing, they inadvertently give him access and reduce their spiritual defenses to a "zero point."

Investment Through Ancestral Links and Covenants

By divine covenant with Abraham, the children of Israel have been invested with the spiritual garments of blessedness from the Lord. A similar ancestral chain of "custody" applies to the Aaronic priesthood; Eleazer inherited the garments of ministry from his father, Aaron (see Exod. 6:23 and Exod. 28:1-4). By the same token, many people live under bondages established by idol-worshiping ancestors. The evil spiritual garments worn because of idolatry are automatically transferred to descendants. The same is true of any evil covenants entered into by past generations; the evil spiritual garments generated by such agreements are invested in generations yet unborn.

For example, those who inherit the evil garments of polygamy will always run into circumstances designed to break up their marriages. The individual circumstances may vary, but the end result is the same. The only solution to this bondage is deliverance; because of the blood of Jesus, the yoke can be broken!

Investment Through Curses

When Jacob was about to die, he called his children together and prophesied to each of them. When he came to Reuben, his eldest son, Jacob prophesied a curse. The curse resulted from Reuben's sinful way of life: he had sexually violated his father's relationship with a concubine named Bilhah (see Gen. 35:22):

Reuben, thou art my firstborn, my might, and the beginning of my strength, the excellency of dignity, and the excellency of power: unstable as water, thou shalt not excel; because thou wentest up to thy father's bed; then defiledst thou it: he went up to my couch (Gen. 49:3-4).

The curse decreed by Jacob clothed Reuben and his descendants in demonic garments that bring failure. Dathan and Abiram, mentioned earlier, were the great grandchildren of Reuben who rebelled against Moses. Perhaps, if they had understood the spiritual garments that hindered them from excelling, they would have supported Moses and not opposed him to their own detriment.

Now Korah, the son of Izhar, the son of Kohath, the son of Levi, and Dathan and Abiram, the sons of Eliab, and On, the son of Peleth, **sons of Reuben**, *took men: and they rose up before Moses, with certain of the children of Israel, two hundred and fifty princes of the assembly, famous in the congregation, men of renown: and they gathered themselves together against Moses and against Aaron, and said unto them, Ye take too much upon you, seeing all the congregation are holy, every one of them, and the Lord is among them: wherefore then lift ye up yourselves above the congregation of the Lord?* (Num. 16:1-3, emphasis added).

These descendants of Reuben were swallowed up by the ground:

And the earth opened her mouth, and swallowed them up, and their houses, and all the men that appertained unto Korah, and all their goods. They, and all that appertained to them, went down alive into the pit, and the earth closed upon them: and they perished from among the congregation (Num. 16:32-33).

Investment Through Satan, Demons, and Human Agents

The garments of hindrance can be forcefully invested by opposing powers. In Deuteronomy 21:13, the Bible speaks of the raiment (or garment) of captivity. In this case, Scripture speaks of the garments worn by those whom the children of Israel took captive. For a captive woman to become the wife of an Israelite, the garment of her captivity had to be removed.

Likewise in the spiritual realm: a person taken captive by Satan or any satanic agent must cry to the Lord for deliverance or remain a captive forever. Just as the Lord ordered the removal of the filthy spiritual garments worn by Joshua the high priest, Satan orders his agents to clothe people with evil spiritual garments. These are typically people who are ignorant of Satan's devices or are at a "zero point" spiritually. Satan can only succeed in this if he has been given legal ground to do so.

Job is a good example of a man in whom Satan invested garments of hindrance. The great force of disease and affliction suffered by Job changed his spiritual garments of honor, riches, and glory to garments of dishonor. Satan inflicted so many attacks on Job as to finally invest him with the spiritual garments of sorrow, so that he despaired of life itself (see Job 3:3).

Yet, Job remained faithful to God and trusted the fact that, despite his great suffering, his Redeemer lived (Job 19:25). Job was delivered and experienced another "wardrobe" change, so that the latter end of his life was more blessed than the beginning (see Job 42:12).

God's covenant with us is far better than the one that covered Job (see Heb. 8:6). For the redeemed, deliverance and a change out of evil spiritual garments is always available! Because we are covered by the blood of the Lamb, we need only call on God, in Jesus' mighty name! (See Jeremiah 33:3.)

Chapter 3

Undefiled Spiritual Garments

Our Lord Jesus spoke of defiled and undefiled garments. As we have seen, defiled garments are evil spiritual garments that provoke hindrance by the adversary and his agents. Undefiled garments are divine garments of blessing. They symbolize holiness and right standing with God.

Let us look at Jesus' words in Revelation 3:4:

Thou hast a few names even in Sardis which have not defiled their garments; and they shall walk with me in white: for they are worthy.

Again, the garments to which our Lord Jesus refers here are spiritual garments. He is speaking of the few believers in the church of Sardis who choose the garments of salvation and avoid the pitfalls of sin. Falling into sin, especially into patterns of sin, causes us to be clothed with defiled garments.

Behold, I come as a thief. Blessed is he that watcheth, and keepeth his garments, lest he walks naked, and they see his shame (Rev. 16:15).

Jesus spoke of garments in relation to our watchfulness for His Second Coming. We are admonished to remain on guard, carefully conducting our lives in righteousness so that we are ready for His return.

The words of our Lord Jesus reveal that individuals can choose to defile their spiritual garments. They can, by physical carelessness and conscious sin, exchange their undefiled garments for garments of hindrance. As serious and consequential as this choice is, such loss is not a foregone conclusion. We can also, by the grace of God and physical vigilance, choose to keep our undefiled garments intact.

According to Revelation 16:15, the defilement of spiritual garments is a form of spiritual nakedness. The wearers of such garments are no longer protected. Instead, they are exposed and shamed; nakedness in the spirit realm can be compared to inappropriate nakedness in the physical realm—it produces shame and vulnerability.

The pure condition of our spiritual garments *can be* sustained. One of the ways we keep our garments white and pure is by following Jesus' instruction to avoid entanglement in the cares of this world (see Mark 4:18-20). Those who remain undefiled by life's "thorns" will bring forth abundant fruit from good ground.

The Undefiled Garments of the Bible

The Bible instructs us often as to the wearing of spiritual garments; it speaks of different kinds of spiritual attire and presents them in a variety of contexts. We will consider first the undefiled spiritual garments that are in keeping with His Word and will for us.

Garments of Salvation

This spiritual garment is fundamental to our relationship with God as followers of Christ. It is the foundational garment, spiritually speaking.

*I will greatly rejoice in the Lord, my soul shall be joyful in my God; for he hath clothed me with the **garments of sal-***

vation, he hath covered me with the robe of righteousness, as a bridegroom decketh himself with ornaments, and as a bride adorneth herself with her jewels (Isa. 61:10, emphasis added).

When an individual accepts Jesus Christ as Lord and Savior, we say there is a *conversion*. In other words, a notable change occurs. The greatest part of this change occurs in the unseen realm of the spirit. However, this level of transformation ultimately affects conduct and outcomes in the natural, physical realm.

One aspect of conversion is an automatic change of spiritual garments: the old, defiled garments are replaced with new garments that are pure and undefiled. As the spirit man is resurrected from death (which is the fruit of sin), the garments of sin are stripped away and replaced by the garments of salvation.

The garments of salvation are what I call the born-again Christian's foundation garments. Those who wear them are clothed with beautiful outer garments, too: the robe of righteousness adorns the born-again child of God. This is the righteousness of God in Christ Jesus, a robe from Christ's own "wardrobe."

White Garments

The Bible admonishes believers to wear white garments, always. Spiritually speaking, they represent holiness of life and heart.

Let thy garments be always white; and let thy head lack no ointment (Eccles. 9:8).

White garments are emblematic of the believer's righteousness in God. Jesus spoke of white garments in Revelation 3:18:

I counsel thee to buy of me gold tried in the fire, that thou mayest be rich; and white raiment [garment]*, that thou mayest be clothed, and that the shame of thy nakedness* *do not appear; and anoint thine eyes with eye salve, that thou mayest see.*

According to the Lord Jesus Christ, white raiment is a kind of clothing that fitly covers us. In other words, it is a genuine garment—one that prevents our being naked. When we are naked, we are exposed to poverty, shame, disfavor, and dishonor.

In the Transfiguration, the Bible provides an unforgettable reminder that the white garments mentioned elsewhere in the Bible are the spiritual garments of the Lord Jesus Christ:

And his raiment became shining, exceeding white as snow; so as no fuller on earth can white them (Mark 9:3).

According to the words of Jesus in His revelation to the apostle John, white spiritual garments constitute the ultimate wardrobe of overcomers:

He that overcometh, the same shall be clothed in white raiment; and I will not blot out his name out of the book of life, but I will confess his name before my Father, and before his angels (Rev. 3:5).

These are the garments of victory and joy. Those who conquer Satan's devices are invested with white garments and enjoy three benefits as a result:

1. Their names are written in the Lamb's book of life.
2. The Lord Jesus confesses their names before God the Father.
3. The Lord Jesus confesses their names before God's angels. That is, Jesus instructs His angels to assist them in times of need or trouble. Praise the Lord!

31

Holy Garments

As God established Israel as a free people en route to the Promised Land, He also provided a great deal of guidance in terms of their place of worship in the wilderness (the Tabernacle), their methods of worship, and the selection and conduct of the priesthood. This instruction included strict guidelines as to the priestly garments reserved for Aaron and his descendants. These garments were to be seen as holy garments.

> *And thou shalt make holy garments for Aaron thy brother for glory and for beauty* (Exod. 28:2).

Today, because of the sacrifice of Christ, all born-again believers are to be clothed in priestly garments, spiritually speaking (see 1 Pet. 2:9 and Rev. 1:6). These are garments of righteousness that bring glory and beauty as they testify of Christ. They reflect the priestly garments given to Aaron and his sons as gifts from the Israelites (see Exod. 35:21). They carry the anointing, which brings favor, blessing, and protection (see Exod. 29:29). They attract prosperity, excellence, and success—as well as God's love, mercy, power, and security.

Garment of Praise:

The prophet Isaiah mentions this garment and explains its purpose:

> *To appoint unto them that mourn in Zion, to give unto them beauty for ashes, the oil of joy for mourning, the garment of praise for the spirit of heaviness; that they might be called trees of righteousness, the planting of the LORD, that he might be glorified* (Isa. 61:3).

The purpose of this garment is very specific: it comes against the spirit of heaviness. This spirit is a demonic power that oppresses the soul in order to create a sense of dejection and discouragement. The garment of praise is an effective weapon; it repels and destroys the spirit of heaviness. When believers wear the garment of praise and begin to worship the Lord in hymns and other worship songs, the spirit of heaviness has no choice but to flee. It acts as a shield or defense against the enemy's attempts to burden and undermine us.

Beautiful Garments

The prophet Isaiah speaks of beautiful garments:

Awake, awake; put on thy strength, O Zion; put on thy beautiful garments, O Jerusalem, the holy city: for henceforth there shall no more come into thee the uncircumcised and the unclean (Isa. 52:1).

Beautiful garments are holy garments that bring glory and attract honor.

Goodly Raiment

In our natural lives, the garments we wear cause others to respond to us in very specific ways. If our clothes are rumpled and soiled, others will tend to attribute to us, as people, the negative qualities of our apparel. They will question our character and cleanliness; they will treat us the way our dress indicates that we treat ourselves.

As is it in the physical, so it is in the spiritual. The "scent" of our spiritual garments can draw or repel favor. The apostle James spoke of *"goodly apparel"* (James 2:2). James referred to the kind of clothing worn by the rich. He warned that, in the physical realm, fine clothing can draw an ungodly form of favoritism. However, goodly raiment can also bring godly favor—both in the physical and spiritual realms.

The implications for our lives are powerful. We should desire and seek to be clothed in the goodly garments that will serve to make us effective ambassadors of Christ. We need to proactively pursue this place of influence for the Kingdom, for the glory of God!

To that end, please stop for a moment and pray this prayer:

Father God, invest me with spiritual garments that speak of Your favor. Clothe me in raiment that will make me a person of honor and influence in my generation, in the name of Jesus. Amen.

The Transfiguration: Jesus' Garments of Purity and Perfection

And after six days Jesus taketh with him Peter, and James, and John, and leadeth them up into an high mountain apart by themselves: and he was transfigured before them. And his raiment became shining, exceeding white as snow; so as no fuller on earth can white them (Mark 9:2-3).

Jesus was transfigured before Peter, James, and John. To transfigure is literally to change figure or appearance. The Lord opened the eyes of the three disciples so they could see Him as He looks in the spirit realm.

The Bible here specifically speaks of the condition or appearance of Jesus' garments. They are described as being as white as snow—so white that no launderer or bleach on earth could produce the same effect. The shining white appearance of Jesus' spiritual garment indicated purity and complete perfection.

Jesus revealed His spiritual garments for the benefit of His disciples. He wanted them to know that these were heavenly garments (see Dan. 7:9) that enabled Him to carry out His earthly assignments unhindered. Had His garments been spotted by the flesh (see Jude 23), they would have brought hindrance (see Rev. 3:4).

Divine garments invested by the Spirit secure success and progress. They attract angelic beings that support genuine undertakings to successful ends. As the filthy garments of Joshua the high priest attracted Satan's effort to hinder, so also do divine garments attract God's angels and other positive forces that support advancement (see Gen. 35:2).

Likewise, defiled garments attract demonic activities to repel and cut off blessing from those to whom it is due. So many believers go about in torn, dirty spiritual clothes without even realizing it. However, many see themselves in dreams in which they are dressed in such clothing. Unfortunately, most people shrug off these divine revelations, proving even more clearly that they are in need of deliverance.

If your living conditions are not glorifying the Lord, if you are beset with hindrances in life, your spiritual garments may be responsible. The only solution is to run to God and seek His deliverance. If you do, He will change your spiritual clothes and you will experience supernatural transformation!

Garments in the Bible

We have mentioned a number of spiritual garments in varying levels of detail. We will discuss specific garments at greater length in Chapter 5.

The following is a general listing of garments named in the Bible. Included in the list are divine garments and garments of hindrance. (Please note that the word *raiment* is frequently used in place of the word *garment* in the King James Version of the Bible.)

1. Goodly raiment (Gen. 27:15; James 2:2)
2. Garment of captivity/bondage (Deut. 21:13)
3. Garment of shame and/or dishonor (Job 8:22; Ps. 35:26; Ps. 109:29)
4. Widow's raiment (Deut. 24:17)
5. Old garment (Josh. 9:5)
6. Prison garment (2 Kings 25:29; Jer. 52:33)
7. White garment (Eccles. 9:8, Matt. 17:2)
8. Beautiful garment (Isaiah 52:1)
9. Holy garment (Exod. 28:1-2; 29:29)
10. Garment of praise (Isa. 61:3)

11. Garment of salvation (Isa. 61:10)
12. Stained raiment (Isa. 63:3)
13. Embroidered garment (Ezek. 16:18)
14. Filthy garment (Zech. 3:3)
15. Rough garment (Zech. 13:4)
16. Wedding garment (Matt. 22:11)
17. Shining raiment (Mark 9:3; Luke 24:4)
18. New garment (Luke 5:36)
19. Grave clothes (John 11:44)
20. Moth-eaten (worn out or outdated) garment (James 5:2)
21. Vile raiment (James 2:2)
22. Priest's garment (Ezra 2:69; Neh. 7:70)
23. Dyed garments (Isa. 63:1)
24. Garments of divers (or various) colors (2 Sam. 13:18)
25. Garment of vengeance (Isa. 59:17) (Please note that only God wears this garment.)
26. Garments spotted by the flesh (Jude 23)
27. Idol worshiper's (occult) garments (Gen. 35:1-7)
28. Attire (garments) of harlots (Prov. 7:10)

Now that we are beginning to develop a sense of the diversity of spiritual garments and the various outcomes they can promote in the spirit realm, let's continue our study by examining some of the forces behind the influence of the spiritual garments we wear.

Chapter 4

The Great Forces Behind Garments of Hindrance

During his trials, Job uttered many words which were carefully recorded in the Bible for our benefit. Among these are words of wisdom and words of knowledge; others are words of revelation, anguish, crying, lamentation, and prophecy.

One such statement by Job was a word of revelation that provided important information regarding the assault on our beautiful garments by great and mighty forces in the spirit realm.

By the great force of my disease is my garment changed: it bindeth me about as the collar of my coat (Job 30:18).

Let me highlight some important excerpts of spiritual significance from this single verse:

1. "By the great force of my disease"
2. "My garment changed"
3. "It bindeth me about"

The phrase *"by the great force"* literally indicates a vigorous, mighty, multiplied source of power, which is in this case an evil power.[1] Although Job refers specifically to the great force of his disease, we know that disease is not the only great force of evil that sets itself against God's people. Other "great forces" desire to besiege us, including the great forces of:

Addictions
Anger
Bitterness
Curses
Deception
Hopelessness
Evil words or pronouncements
Fear
Fornication and adultery
Household wickedness; household enemies—
(*i.e.*, witchcraft or occult practiced in the family)
Infirmity
Lust (invests garments of harlotry)
Poverty
Pride
Sin
Captivity
The occult
The environment (territorial spirits)
Witchcraft
Worry

The clause, *"my garment changed"* from Job 30:18 means that the garment has been made different from what it used to be. Spiritually speaking, it can also mean that a particular garment has been:

Altered
Distorted
Exchanged
Modified
Stained
Torn

Job's undefiled garment was changed by the great force of his disease. His divine garment of joy and honor (which marked his life prior to Satan's attack) was changed to the spiritual garment of lamentation and mourning. Mighty powers of evil, like the Leviathan spirit (see Job 41:1), came against Job; through oppression and affliction, his spiritual garments were changed.

When Job said of his garment that *"it bindeth me about,"* he was literally saying that the garment was belted or wrapped around him.[2] Spiritually, anything that binds, can restrain. Anything that binds, ties up. Anything that binds, restricts movement.

The point here is that spiritual garments can bring us into freedom or bondage, prosperity or lack, fame or obscurity. Such powerful binding may be difficult to cast off unless a more potent force is employed to counter it. In the case of Job, the most potent force in all creation intervened: Almighty God helped Job to put off the evil spiritual garments that had him bound.

The Great Forces That Changed Joseph's Garments

Joseph was an individual whose spiritual garments were changed many times before his dreams came to pass (see Gen. 37:7,9).

In his youth, Joseph's brothers removed the coat of many color given to him by his father, Jacob. The angry siblings probably put another garment on him before they dumped him into a pit to die:

> *And it came to pass, when Joseph was come unto his brethren, that they stript Joseph out of his coat, his coat of many colours that was on him; and they took him, and cast him into a pit: and the pit was empty, there was no water in it* (Gen. 37:23-24).

The great force that changed Joseph's garments involved members of his own family. Because of their jealousy and anger over Joseph's dreams, they became his household enemies. Their actions were designed to prevent his rising above them; in desperation, they changed his coat of many colors to a garment of death, stained with blood (Gen. 37:31-33).

Joseph's brothers then sold him to the Ishmaelite traders, who in turn transported him to Egypt as a slave.

Then there passed by Midianites merchantmen; and they drew and lifted up Joseph out of the pit, and sold Joseph to the Ishmeelites for twenty pieces of silver: and they brought Joseph into Egypt (Gen. 37:28).

Once in Egypt, the traders sold Joseph to Potiphar, an officer of Pharaoh. In Potiphar's household, Joseph served as a slave; he was a man held captive. While wearing the garments of captivity in Potiphar's house, Joseph was pursued by other great forces—fornication and adultery, and even lust.

And it came to pass after these things, that his master's wife cast her eyes upon Joseph; and she said, Lie with me. But he refused, and said unto his master's wife, Behold, my master wotteth not what is with me in the house, and he hath committed all that he hath to my hand; there is none greater in this house than I; neither hath he kept back any thing from me but thee, because thou art his wife: how then can I do this great wickedness, and sin against God? And it came to pass, as she spake to Joseph day by day, that he hearkened not unto her, to lie by her, or to be with her. And it came to pass about this time, that Joseph went into the house to do his business; and there was none of the men of the house there within. And she caught him by his garment, saying, Lie with me: and he left his garment in her hand, and fled, and got him out (Gen. 39:7-12).

Potiphar's wife wanted to have sexual relations with Joseph, but Joseph rejected the offer. Because he turned her down, Potiphar's wife lied about Joseph and accused him of making sexual advances toward her. Joseph was put in prison for the supposed offense.

Through the great forces of fornication and adultery and lust, a new garment was invested in Joseph—a prison garment.

And Joseph's master took him, and put him into the prison, a place where the king's prisoners were bound: and he was there in the prison (Gen. 39:20).

Although Joseph was unjustly cast into prison, the Bible reveals that God was with him and made a way for him to succeed, even in the dungeon.

But the LORD was with Joseph, and shewed him mercy, and gave him favour in the sight of the keeper of the prison (Gen. 39:21).

Joseph suffered the harshness of an unjust incarceration. After being seemingly forgotten and forsaken, God made a way for Joseph to fulfill His divine purpose. Joseph correctly interpreted Pharaoh's dreams and, as a result, Pharaoh raised Joseph to a high place as second in command of mighty Egypt.

And Pharaoh took off his ring from his hand, and put it upon Joseph's hand, and arrayed him in vestures of fine linen, and put a gold chain about his neck; (Gen. 41:42).

Joseph's garments were changed yet again, from prison garments to vestures of fine linen, or beautiful garments. The greatest force of all, the force of Almighty God transformed Joseph's wardrobe and his life!

God can do a similar work in your life. He can change your clothes and thereby change your life. The Bible tells us to ask, seek, and knock (see Matt. 7:7). Let's pause for a moment as you ask the Lord in prayer to exchange your defiled garments for beautiful new ones:

O Lord, by the greatness of Your power, I ask that You change my soiled garments to beautiful garments, in the name of Jesus.

Jehoiachin, the King of Judah Changed Garments

Jehoiachin was eight years on the throne of Judah when King Nebuchadnezzar attacked Jerusalem and carried him away to Babylon as a prisoner of war (see 2 Kings 24:12). Jehoiachin remained in prison for 37 years in the land of Babylon.

The great force of King Nebuchadnezzar changed the royal garments of King Jehoiachin into prison garments. Yet, after 37 years, a far greater force replaced those garments with beautiful garments: Almighty God Himself used the new Babylonian king, Evil-merodach, to change Jehoiachin's garments once more.

Evil-merodach released Jehoiachin king of Judah from prison. The Bible says his prison garments were changed, and he began to wine and to dine with the king of Babylon until the day he died (see 2 Kings 25:27-29).

Before we continue, please pause once again and pray these prayers for your own life:

1. Lord Jesus, assign Your angels to remove the spiritual garments of captivity invested in me by the great forces of darkness.
2. Lord Jesus, assign Your angels to invest me now with new divine garments of liberty, as You did for Jehoiachin.
3. Thank You, Jesus, for my new garments!

It should be noted that all the physical changes that are recorded above actually took place first in the spirit realm, before any physical manifestations were evident. By this, I mean that the spiritual garments were set in place before the physical garments manifested.

The Greater Forces That Invest Goodly Garments

These greater forces are the spiritual forces that are able to remove any garment of hindrance and instantly invest an individual with goodly spiritual garments in their place. These are the spiritual forces that believers ought to invoke continually in order to remain dressed in spiritual garments of white.

1. **The force of the name of the Lord.** Proverbs 18:10 says, *"The name of the LORD is a strong tower: the righteous runneth into it, and is safe."* We are to keep His name on our tongues and remain sheltered in Him.

2. **The force of the Holy Spirit and power.** When the Holy Spirit came upon the apostles and other disciples on the day of Pentecost (see Acts 2), the great forces of fear and lying were consumed. Boldness was manifested in their utterances from that moment on.

3. **The force of the blood of Jesus.** Revelation 12:11 says: *"And they overcame him by the blood of the Lamb, and by the word of their testimony; and they loved not their lives unto the death"* (emphasis added). The blood of Jesus is our ultimate covering!

4. **The force of the word of believers' testimony.** *"And they overcame him by the blood of the Lamb, and by the word of their testimony; and they loved not their lives unto the death"* (Rev. 12:11, emphasis added). Our testimony before others weaves a garment of praise!

5. **The force of Christ's salvation.** *"For God hath not appointed us to wrath, but to obtain salvation by our Lord Jesus Christ..."* (1 Thess. 5:9). Christ's salvation is a force that invests the foundational garment; salvation keeps us in His care and Kingdom and empowers us to receive from Him.

6. The force of the Word of the Lord. Psalms 33:6 tells us: *"By the word of the LORD were the heavens made; and all the host of them by the breath of his mouth."* Psalms 148:7-8 says: *"Praise the LORD from the earth, ye dragons, and all deeps: fire, and hail; snow, and vapor; stormy wind fulfilling his word...."* The Word of God invests us with wisdom and understanding and empowers us for warfare.

7. The force of righteousness. *"Righteousness exalteth a nation: but sin is a reproach to any people"* (Prov. 14:34). The robe of righteousness overwhelms every garment of hindrance as we trust in Him and all He has done for us.

A believer who knows how to walk in these truths and apply these greater forces will thrive no matter the opposition. He or she will overtake and destroy the forces that desire to keep us dressed in garments of hindrance!

Endnotes

1. Biblesoft's New Exhaustive Strong's Numbers and Concordance with Expanded Greek-Hebrew Dictionary. CD-ROM. Biblesoft, Inc. and International Bible Translators, Inc. s.v. "koach," (OT 3581) and s.v. "rab," (OT 7227).

2. Ibid., s.v. " 'azar," (OT 247).

Chapter 5

Specific Garments of Hindrance

It is time to examine in greater detail several garments that hinder and oppress. These are defiled or evil spiritual garments with specific recognizable characteristics. The better equipped we are to identify these garments, the more empowered we are to remove them and replace them with the undefiled garments of the Kingdom.

Garments Spotted by the Flesh

The Bible speaks of defiled garments that are spotted by the flesh:

And others save with fear, pulling them out of the fire; hating even the garment spotted by the flesh (Jude 23).

Something that is spotted bears an external mark or blemish.[1] Therefore, a spotted garment represents that which is external—specifically, our carnal desires. This verse from Jude speaks of a godly person who is invested with goodly garments that have been stained by the cares of the flesh and the cares of this world. Those who wear such garments battle the evil syndrome of being "almost there" but never quite arriving. Unless the issue of the spotted garment is reconciled and the righteousness of the goodly garment is chosen over the stains, these believers will never achieve what they were called to do (see Isa. 61:10).

Occult Garments

Those who have been involved in the occult, but are now seeking a new life in Christ must understand that they have been invested with the spiritual garments of the occult. They must seek the Lord to remove these garments of hindrance; they must do so as tenaciously as they seek to be invested with the garments of salvation that He provides.

Occult garments are often handed down from past generations of occult members. Unless the Word of God is appropriated and applied against this evil investiture, the person lacking knowledge will be hindered (see Hos. 4:6 and Isa. 5:13).

While on his way to Bethel, Jacob asked members of his household to put off their garments of idol worship so they would not be hindered or opposed on their journey (see Gen. 35:1-7). He wisely purged his house (his family); he knew that garments of idol worship would expose them to demonic attack and hinder their God-ordained mission.

Filthy Garments

You will remember the story of Joshua the high priest discussed in Chapter 2. Joshua had a "hindrance encounter" with Satan. Because of sin, Joshua was invested with filthy garments. That is what sin does—it clothes us in defilement. Filthy garments in turn attract Satan and his agents to hinder us, because the garments provide legal ground from which to do so.

To leave filthy garments intact is to invite poverty, lack, and failure, therefore, Joshua's iniquity was dealt with by God and the filthy garments were removed. Our remedy today is to ask for forgiveness of all sin and plead the blood of Jesus, so that the devil and his agents can no longer hinder our ability to receive blessing from the Lord.

Prison Garments

You have already studied aspects of this spiritual garment in Chapters 3 and 4 (see 2 Kings 25:29 and Jer. 52:33). Spiritual prison garments are garments of bondage; wearers of these garments live in such a way that their lives are not their own. They find themselves subject to various forms of tyranny, including addictions of all sorts. These people also tend to manifest a constant, very negative stubbornness. Their lives reflect this quality through stagnation and resistance to positive change. Demons of limitation and oppression are readily attracted to those who wear prison garments. By God's grace and because of the blood of Jesus, we need not remain clothed in them!

Garments of Captivity

As mentioned in Chapters 2 and 3, spiritual garments of captivity are garments of subjection. Deuteronomy 21:13 speaks of those subjected by Israel as they conquered the Promised Land. In order for a captive woman to become the wife of an Israelite, her garments of captivity had to be removed.

A person invested with garments of captivity cannot be said to be in control of his or her own life. Under this type of oppression, an individual is forced to yield to decisions made by someone else and loses their sense of self-identity.

Garments of Death and the Grave

When Lazarus (a dear friend of Jesus) died, he was wrapped in grave clothes (garments of death and the grave), and then buried. Jesus came and raised him from death after four days in the tomb. Although Lazarus was made alive again, he remained bound—hands, feet, and face—in his death garments (see John 11:44).

Anyone spiritually invested with grave clothes through any great force of wickedness will be bound in the hands, feet, and face. The implication in the physical realm is that...

1. The hands (the symbol of labor) cannot prosper at work.
2. The feet which God has empowered to establish man's dominion on earth cannot function (see Deut. 11:24).
3. Such an individual cannot be a person of vision, as the face has been bound.

A Garment for God Only

The Bible mentions a garment that no man can wear: it is the garment of vengeance.

For he put on righteousness as a breastplate, and an helmet of salvation upon his head; and he put on the garments of vengeance for clothing, and was clad with zeal as a cloak (Isa. 59:17).

No wonder God declares:

To me belongeth vengeance, and recompense; their foot shall slide in due time: for the day of their calamity is at hand, and the things that shall come upon them make haste (Deut. 32:35).

The Word of the Lord expressly prohibits us from wearing the garment of vengeance. It is His alone.

The Results of Wearing Garments of Hindrance

We have seen examples from the Bible and from everyday life of what happens when we remain clothed in garments of hindrance. Let's now summarize the broad categories of negative outcomes that can be attributed toward the wearing of such garments.

1. Garments of hindrance attract the attention of the adversary and serve to focus his attempts to steal, kill, and destroy (see John 10:10) upon those who wear those

garments. Satan will always contend with the righteous desires of those who are so clothed, regardless of their good intentions and desire to serve the Lord.

2. Garments of hindrance attract hindering spirits. No matter where they are, no matter who has purposed to help them, no matter their qualifications, hindering spirits will oppose the success of those arrayed in garments of hindrance. The story of two sons told by the Lord Jesus in Luke 15 is a good example of this truth. The Lord said that *"no man gave unto him* [the prodigal son]*"* (Luke 15:16). Because he wore garments of hindrance, the young son was hindered from receiving from others. In everyday life, we see people who are far more qualified than their competitors, yet fail to succeed. Hindering spirits can operate behind the scenes, causing us to oversleep and miss important appointments or suffer memory loss and forget important promises to and from others. Seemingly insignificant instances like this can take their toll on the opportunities God arranges for us to prosper.

3. Garments of hindrance attract evil pursuers. There are many people who find that, wherever they go, there is an antagonist—someone who dislikes them for no apparent reason. People afflicted in this way search for "logical" explanations for this phenomenon. Often, they grasp at straws or rationalize that these attacks are based on race, language, education, gender, or appearance. Careful investigation into ancestral lineage and other spiritual factors, would unveil the true cause of such harassment. When the garments of hindrance are identified and removed, the pattern is reversed.

4. Garments of hindrance give legitimacy to the activities of ancestral spirits. These spirits demand payment from descendants for the failings of their ancestors. Ancestral spirits base their attacks on the legal ground

established through evil covenants, evil deeds, and evil vows made by past generations.

5. Garments of hindrance give legal ground to territorial spirits to prevail in battle. Evil spirits are committed to the fulfillment of their missions of wickedness. Therefore, they desire to capitalize on every opportunity to carry out their satanic assignments. Garments of hindrance offer just such opportunity. Without the knowledge and wisdom needed to identify and remove these garments of hindrance, the believer is likely to endure endless harassment by territorial spirits (see Isa. 5:13).

As children of the Most High God, we have been granted complete access to the divine "wardrobe." Whatever garments of hindrance we may be wearing, they were scheduled for removal 2,000 years ago! As we continue to learn about the garments of the spirit realm, bear in mind that our goal—and God's promise—is deliverance!

Endnote

1. Biblesoft's New Exhaustive Strong's Numbers and Concordance with Expanded Greek-Hebrew Dictionary. CD-ROM. Biblesoft, Inc. and International Bible Translators, Inc. s.v. "spiloo," (NT 4695) and s.v. "spilos," (NT4696).

Chapter 6

Signs of the Garments of Hindrance

By the Holy Spirit, we are able to discern the presence and nature of the spiritual garments we wear. We discern, not to condemn ourselves or others, but so that we can resist the enemy and any form of evil.

Often, we assume that situations and circumstances are random—that "things are what they are." However, we need to recognize that patterns in life are subject to change and can provide the clues we need to expose the ways of darkness.

If we understand that our circumstances often reflect the spiritual garments we wear, then we are empowered to change our garments and, therefore, our lives!

The following are examples of patterns and circumstances that may reveal the working of garments of hindrance.

1. **When living a normal life becomes difficult.** A life that is under the continual siege of problems, crises, and emergencies, cannot be stable. These kinds of situations baffle and defy remedy. Often, people in such situations haven't a clue as to how it started or whether it will ever end. Included are strange experiences and "abnormal" situations that occur for no apparent

reason, such as the sudden end of a key friendship or the souring of a beneficial relationship.

2. **When there is little or no progress in life.** For many in this category, life seems stalled. After years of struggle, effort, and application, they have little to show for it. Progress continually fails to meet expectations. As a result, these individuals become disenchanted, begin to complain, and leave in hopes of a better opportunity elsewhere. Instead, they find themselves continually starting over and unable to make substantial headway.

3. **When life is "circular."** For some, life seems always to be moving in a circle. Things start off well, but end badly, with unexpected glitches or obstacles forcing a downturn. People caught in circular living often experience failure at the very cusp of breakthrough. Plans and efforts, however well-laid and sincere, are aborted.

4. **When there is inexplicable hatred.** For those struggling with hatred from an unrecognized source, there is little that turns out right. Seething hatred hinders the flow of favor and keeps the person from moving forward. Hopes are routinely dashed and one disappointment follows another, ensuring ongoing cycles of misery.

5. **When there is poverty and fruitless labor.** Often, those invested with garments of hindrance do not eat the fruits of their labor, even though they are working. Beneficial "transactions" (including relational, ministry, financial, and emotional experiences) reach the point of benefit, but then shift away due to unforeseen problems or obstacles. Such people often go for many years without a raise in pay. When they express their dissatisfaction, they are fired. Too often, those wearing garments of hindrance receive no reward for their dili-

gence at work. They are routinely offered low-end jobs rather than the more rewarding positions for which they qualify.

6. **When one is unable to serve God genuinely.** Anyone afflicted with garments of hindrance will experience hindrance in their service to the Lord, just as Joshua the high priest was hindered in performing his priestly duties (see Zech. 3:1-3). Genuine spiritual purposes will routinely be derailed, resulting in the diversion of energy to useless activities. Spiritual growth is also hampered; although much effort is applied advancement, spiritually and otherwise, is stymied.

7. **When the life span of positive experiences and situations is cut short.** Common symptoms of unnatural abbreviation include: a pattern of short stretches at good jobs, good relationships that fail to last, the sudden end of profitable ventures, and the premature evaporation of favorable expectations. When a pattern of abbreviation emerges, the wearing of garments of hindrance should be suspected and searched out in prayer.

8. **When there is a constant desire to do wrong things.** Any pattern of compulsion to do wrong should raise awareness that garments of hindrance may be at work.

How Garments of Hindrance Are Removed

When we detect the investment of garments of hindrance, we must remember that we have the authority to strip ourselves of them. In Christ, we are never defenseless against evil. We need only resist evil by the Spirit of God, as those who are covered by the blood of Jesus.

We can remove untoward spiritual garments:

1. **Through personal decision.** When we recognize patterns of unfavorable circumstances, we can rise up in

the power of the Lord and *decide* to undo the works of the enemy. Second Timothy 4:18 says:

The Lord shall deliver me from every evil work,
and will preserve me unto his heavenly kingdom:
to whom be glory forever and ever. Amen.

The Lord is always ready; we need only make the decision to be delivered from any garment of hindrance and He will deliver us from evil.

In Luke 15:11-24, Jesus told the story of a wealthy man with two sons. The younger son requested his portion of the father's wealth. The father obliged and gave the son his inheritance.

Already possessed by a waster (or *squandering* spirit), the young man moved to another city and squandered his portion (see Isa. 54:16 and Prov. 18:9). The Bible records that, after a time of suffering and eating food meant for swine, the young man regained his senses. He repented and purposed to return to his father.

In other words, the young man *made a decision* to remove the garments of hindrance invested in him by the great force of reckless spending. When he reached home, the first thing his father did was to change the son's garments. The father asked that the best robe be immediately draped on him.

But the father said to his servants, Bring forth the best
robe, and put it on him; and put a ring on his hand, and
shoes on his feet... (Luke 15:22).

This robe reflected the father's attitude toward his boy. Without a change of clothing, the young man would not have accessed the blessings of his father's house. The servants would have seen him as one of them, or as a rejected and unwanted son.

The young son's decision to remove the garment of hindrance invested in him by the great force of reckless spending was a choice—an *effective* choice.

2. **Through the confession and repentance of personal sins and the iniquity of ancestors.** The so-called prodigal son's story told by the Lord Jesus in Luke 15 clearly shows the power in confessing and repenting of wrongdoing before the Lord. The son stood before his compassionate father and confessed the error of his ways. This immediately prompted the father to act and change his garments.

> *And he arose, and came to his father. But when he was yet a great way off, his father saw him, and had compassion, and ran, and fell on his neck, and kissed him. And the son said unto him, Father, I have sinned against heaven, and in thy sight, and am no more worthy to be called thy son. But the father said to his servants, Bring forth the best robe, and put it on him; and put a ring on his hand, and shoes on his feet:* (Luke 15:20-22; see also Ezra 9:5-10).

3. **Through divine intervention.** God Almighty intervened personally to quash the resistance put forward by Satan against Joshua the high priest because of his spiritual filthy garments. Our Lord is compassionate and will defend His interest in any person who has received His favor through the sacrifice of His Son.

4. **Through habitual living in holiness by the Holy Spirit.** When one habitually lives in holiness by the power of the Holy Spirit, garments of hindrance cannot be invested. Instead, such people will be invested with the goodly spiritual garments associated with walking in God's ways.

5. **Through intensive prayer.** A serious prayer program will reveal one's spiritual garments. Further intensive

prayer will remove any garment of hindrance that has been invested.

6. **Through deliverance ministration.** Those who see themselves (in a dream or vision) wearing dirty or torn or stained clothes, must seek deliverance immediately. Jesus is ready to deliver those who come to Him in the spirit of humility to be set free from the yoke of garments of hindrance. Just as God delivered Joshua the high priest, He will deliver us.

Obadiah 17 says: *"But upon mount Zion shall be deliverance, and there shall be holiness; and the house of Jacob shall possess their possessions."*

We were not created to live in captivity. Nor do we serve a God who is ambivalent toward our situations. He is faithful to reveal the condition and nature of our spiritual garments; and He is mighty to dress us in His best robe—the robe of His righteousness!

Chapter 7

Prayers to Overcome the Great Forces Behind Garments of Hindrance

N ow that we have laid the groundwork and understand key aspects of our spiritual "wardrobes," we are ready, through prayer, to strip away specific garments of hindrance.

We begin by dealing with the great forces that cause these garments to be invested in the first place. Ask the Holy Spirit to reveal the activities of these great forces in your life. You will then be equipped, through prayer, to divest yourself of the evil garments associated with them.

Please note that, in all prayers presented throughout this handbook, we are dealing with spiritual garments, not physical ones.

✝ Prayers to Deal With the Great Force of Fear

Fear is a cruel taskmaster. This demonic force is designed to distract and destroy. Until fear is uncovered and demolished, it will encourage compromise and jeopardize personal destiny.

BIBLE LINKS TO PRAYER GUIDES

For ye have not received the spirit of bondage again to fear; but ye have received the Spirit of adoption, whereby we cry, Abba, Father (Rom. 8:15).

Be not afraid of sudden fear, *neither of the desolation of the wicked, when it cometh* (Prov. 3:25, emphasis added).

So that we may boldly say, The Lord is my helper, and I will not fear what man shall do unto me (Heb. 13:6).

For God hath not given us the spirit of fear; but of power, and of love, and of a sound mind (2 Tim. 1:7).

PRAYER FOCUS

- To be divested of any garment of hindrance generated by the great force of fear
- To neutralize the activities of the great force of fear intended to produce and invest a garment of hindrance
- To use the greater divine forces that are available to neutralize the great force of fear

PRAYER GUIDES

1. Purpose to enter this prayer program with a heart of spiritual violence to take or remove by force (see Matt. 11:12).

2. Pray: "O Lord, in the name of Jesus, forgive my sins and the sins of my ancestors that have invested me with any garments of hindrance."

3. Plead the blood of Jesus over every confessed sin.

4. Rebuke in the name of Jesus, demons that have been operating against your life due to any of the sins you have just confessed.

5. Now begin the prayers of thanksgiving to the Lord for His past benefits, His present care, and His future blessings for you.

6. Declare: "Any garment of hindrance invested in me by the great force of fear, I take you off now, by the power of the Holy Spirit, in the name of Jesus."

7. Declare: "By the Spirit of the Lord in me, I overcome the great force of fear assigned to invest me with a garment of hindrance, in the name of Jesus."

8. Declare: "By the blood of the Lamb of God, I subdue the great force of fear projected against me by Satan and contrived to invest me with a garment of hindrance."

9. Pray: "O Lord, by the greater force of Holy Spirit power, I counter and suppress the activities of the great force of fear in my life."

10. Declare: "I command, by my authority in the third heaven, that any satanic agent assigning the great force of fear to me (in order to invest me with the garment of captivity), to loose his power, in Jesus' name."

11. Declare: "By the greater force of the blood of Jesus and the word of my testimony, I overcome the great force of fear projected against my life by any witch or wizard" (see Rev. 12:11).

12. Declare: "In the name of Jesus, I refuse to wear any garment of captivity prepared for me by the great force of fear."

13. Pray: "Lord Jesus, empower me by the Holy Spirit to neutralize the great force of sudden fear contrived to invest me with a garment of hindrance."

14. Declare: "By the power in the name of Jesus, I release my soul from the violent attack of the great force of sudden fear designed to invest me with any garment of hindrance."

15. Declare: "I command every projected great force of fear fashioned to invest me with a garment of hindrance to go back to its sender, in the name of Jesus."

16. Pray: "Blood of Jesus, divest me of any garment of hindrance forcefully put on me by the great force of fear, in the name of Jesus."

17. Pray and thank the Lord for your victory in this prayer program.

✝ PRAYERS TO DEAL WITH THE GREAT FORCE OF ANGER

As you pray, be aware that anger is directly linked to fear. Seek the wisdom of the Holy Spirit in uncovering areas of anger and in discovering their roots in fear.

BIBLE LINKS TO PRAYER GUIDES

Simeon and Levi are brethren; instruments of cruelty are in their habitations. O my soul, come not thou into their secret; unto their assembly, mine honor, be not thou united: for in their anger they slew a man, and in their selfwill they digged down a wall. Cursed be their anger, for it was fierce; and their wrath, for it was cruel: I will divide them in Jacob, and scatter them in Israel (Gen. 49:5-7).

And it came to pass, as soon as he came nigh unto the camp, that he saw the calf, and the dancing: and Moses' anger waxed hot, and he cast the tables out of his hands, and brake them beneath the mount (Exod. 32:19).

Be not hasty in thy spirit to be angry: for anger resteth in the bosom of fools (Eccles. 7:9).

A soft answer turneth away wrath: but grievous words stir up anger (Prov. 15:1).

PRAYER FOCUS

• To neutralize grievous, hurtful words that stir up the great force of anger
•To curse the great force of anger that invests murderous garments

PRAYER GUIDES

1. Purpose to enter this prayer program with a heart of spiritual violence to take or remove by force (see Matt. 11:12).

2. Pray: "O Lord, in the name of Jesus, forgive my sins and the sins of my ancestors that have invested me with any garment of hindrance."

3. Plead the blood of Jesus over every confessed sin.

4. Rebuke in the name of Jesus, demons that have been operating against your life due to any of the sins you have just confessed.

5. Now begin the prayers of thanksgiving to the Lord for His past benefits, His present care, and His future blessings for you.

6. Declare: "Great force of anger launched by the words of the mouth and assigned to destroy me, I curse you now and command you to go back to the sender, in the name of Jesus."

7. Declare: "Grievous words assigned to stir up fierce anger within me in order to invest me with a garment of hindrance, be cast down, in the name of Jesus."

8. Pray: "Let the blood of Jesus stand against and neutralize the evil words projected to stir up the great force of anger in my life, in the name of Jesus."

9. Declare: "In the name of Jesus, the great force of anger shall not cover me with any garment of hindrance."

10. Pray: "Father God, arise for my sake, forgive my sins and the sins of my ancestors, and change my spiritual garments to favor me."

11. Pray: "O Lord, by the blood of Jesus and in His name, destroy the effect of any evil spiritual garment worn by my ancestors and invested in me."

12. Pray: "Let the fire of God burn to ashes any garment of hindrance shaped and prepared for my use by the great force of inherited anger, in the name of Jesus."

13. Declare: "In the name of Jesus, I command any inherited garment of hindrance originating in the fierce anger of my ancestors to burn to ashes."

14. Declare: "Inherited great force of anger battling my destiny, I curse you to die, in the name of Jesus."

15. Declare: "In the name of Jesus, I bind and cast out anything in me that is cooperating with the great force of anger to keep me invested with any garment of hindrance."

16. Declare: "In the name of Jesus, I destroy the potent power of the great force of anger to invest me with any garment of hindrance."

17. Pray and thank the Lord for your victory in this prayer program.

✞ PRAYERS TO DEAL WITH THE GREAT FORCE OF CURSES

Galatians 3:13 says, *"Christ hath redeemed us from the curse of the law, being made a curse for us...."* It is, however, possible for us to curse ourselves (*i.e.*, through self-condemning words) or to accept curses from others (*i.e.*, ancestral curses or word curses spoken against us).

Through the shed blood of Jesus, we have authority over every form of curse.

BIBLE LINK TO PRAYER GUIDES

*Reuben, thou art my firstborn, my might, and the beginning of my strength, the excellency of dignity, and the excellency of power: unstable as water, **thou shalt not excel;** because thou wentest up to thy father's bed; then defiledst thou it: he went up to my couch* (Gen. 49:3-4, emphasis added).

PRAYER FOCUS

- To terminate the potency of the great force of curses investing a person with a garment of hindrance
- To neutralize the operation of the great force of curses in a life
- To terminate the liveliness of the great force of curses

PRAYER GUIDES

1. Purpose to enter this prayer program with a heart of spiritual violence to take or remove by force (see Matt. 11:12).

2. Pray: "O Lord, in the name of Jesus, forgive my sins and the sins of my ancestors that have invested me with evil garments of failure."

3. Plead the blood of Jesus over every confessed sin.

4. Rebuke in the name of Jesus, demons that have been operating against your life due to any of the sins you have just confessed.

5. Now begin the prayers of thanksgiving to the Lord for His past benefits, His present care, and His future blessings for you.

6. Pray: "O Lord Jesus, if there is in my foundation a curse that says, 'You shall not excel,' neutralize it with Your blood."

7. Declare: "I break the power of any curse issued against me by any demonic agent, in the name of Jesus."

8. Pray: "Holy Spirit, deliver me from the curse of 'You shall not excel' that invested me with a garment of

hindrance which, in turn, chased away from me divine helpers, in the name of Jesus."

9. Declare: "I paralyze, with the power of the Holy Spirit, any demon overseeing any curse in my life, in the name of Jesus."

10. Pray: "I receive divine power and the Holy Spirit anointing to break the power of any curse operating against my destiny, in the name of Jesus."

11. Declare: "In the name of Jesus, I break and loose myself from any inherited curse that is afflicting my destiny (marriage, glory, job, etc.)."

12. Declare: "In the name of Jesus, I break and loose myself from any generational curse that has directly invested me with a garment of hindrance."

13. Declare: "All good things in life that have eluded me because of any curse: I recover you now—in your entirety—in the name of Jesus."

14. Declare: "In the name of Jesus, I break the hold of any curse upon my destiny and I begin to possess my possession."

15. Pray: "Thank You, Jesus, for setting me free from the hold of the great force of curses."

✟ PRAYERS TO DEAL WITH THE GREAT FORCE OF AFFLICTION

Bear in mind that affliction (tribulation, trial, or misfortune) of any kind does more than cause discomfort, pain, and suffering. Affliction is designed to constrain the overall progress of your life and hinder the unfolding of God's plan for you.

Joseph realized that the great force of affliction had invested him with prison garments in the land of Egypt. Moses realized that, because of the pressure of the great force of affliction, the Jews cried unto the Lord and were heard by Him.

BIBLE LINKS TO PRAYER GUIDES

*And she vowed a vow, and said, O LORD of hosts, if thou wilt indeed look **on the affliction** of thine handmaid, and remember me, and not forget thine handmaid, but wilt give unto thine handmaid a man child, then I will give him unto the LORD all the days of his life, and there shall no razor come upon his head* (1 Sam. 1:11, emphasis added).

*And say, Thus saith the king, Put this fellow in the prison, and feed him with **bread of affliction and with water of affliction,** until I come in peace* (1 Kings 22:27, emphasis added).

And the name of the second called he Ephraim: for God hath caused me to be fruitful in the land of my affliction (Gen. 41:52).

And when we cried unto the LORD God of our fathers, the LORD heard our voice, and looked on our affliction, and our labor, and our oppression... (Deut. 26:7).

And when he was in affliction, he besought the Lord his God, and humbled himself greatly before the God of his fathers, (2 Chron. 33:12).

PRAYER FOCUS

• To cry to the Lord for deliverance from the hold of the great force of affliction imposed by oppression and misfortune

• To remove any garment of hindrance that originated from the onslaught of the great force of affliction

PRAYER GUIDES

1. Purpose to enter this prayer program with a heart of spiritual violence to take or remove by force (see Matt. 11:12).

2. Pray: "O Lord, in the name of Jesus, forgive my sins and the sins of my ancestors that have invested me with evil garments of hindrance."

3. Plead the blood of Jesus over every confessed sin.

4. Rebuke in the name of Jesus, demons that have been operating against your life due to any of the sins you have just confessed.

5. Now begin the prayers of thanksgiving to the Lord for His past benefits, His present care, and His future blessings for you.

6. Declare: "Powers assigned to sustain the hold of the great force of affliction on my life and destiny, be paralyzed, in the name of Jesus."

7. Declare: "Spiritual garments of lamentation invested in me by the great force of affliction, be torn to pieces now, in the name of Jesus."

8. Declare: "Spiritual garments of sorrow invested in me by the great force of affliction, catch fire and burn to ashes, in Jesus' name."

9. Pray: "O Lord, deliver me from the siege of the great force of affliction assigned by powers of witchcraft to

invest me with vile spiritual garments, in the name of Jesus."

10. Declare: "Powers assigned to feed me with the bread of affliction, be paralyzed, in the name of Jesus."

11. Declare: "Powers assigned to make me drink the water of affliction, be paralyzed, in the name of Jesus" (see Isa. 30:20).

12. Declare: "Any evil spiritual garment manufactured by the great force of affliction and purposed for my wearing, catch fire and burn to ashes" (see Ps. 88:9).

13. Pray: "Holy Ghost fire, dissolve the bitter affliction that has cut off from me divine helpers, in the name of Jesus" (see 2 Kings 14:26).

14. Declare: "Every affliction fashioned against my life by occult powers to kill my joy and invest me with spiritual garments of sorrow, backfire in the name of Jesus."

15. Declare: "Affliction of shame, expire in my life now, in the name of Jesus."

16. Declare: "Affliction of poverty, expire in my life now, in the name of Jesus."

17. Declare: "Any demonic power generating bitter affliction against my life, be paralyzed, in the name of Jesus."

18. Pray and thank the Lord for your victory in this prayer program.

✞ Prayers to Deal With the Great Force of Disease and Infirmity

As is true of the great force of affliction, disease and infirmity impact not only the physical state of the individual, but the entire life. Thankfully, we can be set free from this demonic force, in the name of Jesus!

Bible Links to Prayer Guides

By the great force of my disease is my garment changed: it bindeth me about as the collar of my coat (Job 30:18, emphasis added).

In those days was Hezekiah sick unto death. And the prophet Isaiah the son of Amoz came to him, and said unto him, Thus saith the Lord, Set thine house in order; for thou shalt die, and not live....And Isaiah said, Take a lump of figs. And they took and laid it on the boil, and he recovered (2 Kings 20:1, 7).

*And Asa in the thirty and ninth year of his reign was **diseased in his feet, until his disease was exceeding great:** yet in his disease he sought not to the Lord, but to the physicians. And Asa slept with his fathers, and died in the one and fortieth year of his reign* (2 Chron. 16:12-13, emphasis added).

Prayer Focus

• To seek deliverance from the hold of the great force of disease and infirmity
• To deal with the great force of disease and infirmity that changes spiritual garments
• To break off from the body the hold of the great force of disease and infirmity

PRAYER GUIDES

1. Purpose to enter this prayer program with a heart of spiritual violence to take or remove by force (see Matt. 11:12).

2. Pray: "O Lord, in the name of Jesus, forgive my sins and the sins of my ancestors that have invested me with any garment of hindrance."

3. Plead the blood of Jesus over every confessed sin.

4. Rebuke in the name of Jesus, demons that have been operating against your life due to any of the sins you have just confessed.

5. Now begin the prayers of thanksgiving to the Lord for His past benefits, His present care, and His future blessings for you.

6. Declare: "As I seek the Lord for my deliverance from the hold of the great force of disease and infirmity, I shall recover from my disease and the evil spiritual garment of sorrow shall be removed from me, in the name of Jesus."

7. Pray: "O Lord, let the spiritual garments of mourning created by the great force of disease and infirmity depart from me now, in the name of Jesus."

8. Pray: "O Lord, in the name of Jesus, remove from me now the garment of hindrance shaped by the great force of disease and infirmity to bind me about" (see Job 30:18).

9. Declare: "In the name of Jesus, I remove the spiritual garments of death invoked on me by the great force of incurable disease and infirmity."

10. Declare: "In the name of Jesus, I receive divine solutions, as King Hezekiah did (see 2 Kings 20:6-7), to neutralize the effect of the great force of disease and infirmity on my body."

11. Declare: "I command any demon that is energizing disease or infirmity in my body to be paralyzed now with the blood of Jesus."

12. Declare: "In the name of Jesus, let every disease or infirmity assigned to my body by any demonic power be neutralized now with the fire of the Holy Ghost."

13. Pray: "Holy Ghost fire, destroy the habitation of any disease or infirmity in my body, to the glory of the Lord."

14. Pray: "O Lord, let the great force of disease and infirmity assigned to change my beautiful garments, expire now, in the name of Jesus."

15. Pray: "Let the healing power in the blood of Jesus come against and destroy any disease or infirmity in my body and make me whole."

16. Pray: "Thank You, Jesus, for healing me of all forms of disease and infirmity."

✝ PRAYERS TO DEAL WITH THE GREAT FORCE OF PRIDE

Isaiah 14:12-14 gives an account of the pride of Lucifer, who sought to establish himself in the place of God. Isaiah 14 goes on to describe the downfall that pride precipitates.

By the grace of God and through prayer, we can establish ourselves in humility and avoid not only the sin of pride, but all of the sin pride fosters.

Bible Links to Prayer Guides

Thou shalt hide them in the secret of thy presence from the pride of man: thou shalt keep them secretly in a pavilion from the strife of tongues (Ps. 31:20).

Let not the foot of pride come against me, and let not the hand of the wicked remove me (Ps. 36:11).

For all that is in the world, the lust of the flesh, and the lust of the eyes, and the pride of life, is not of the Father, but is of the world (1 John 2:16).

Prayer Focus

- To counter the activities of the great force of pride with a humble spirit
- To break the power of pride and prevent it from investing any garment of hindrance
- To kill pride and receive life through the anointing of the grace of humility

Prayer Guides

1. Purpose to enter this prayer program with a heart of spiritual violence to take or remove by force (see Matt. 11:12).

2. Pray: "O Lord, in the name of Jesus, forgive my sins and the sins of my ancestors that have invested me with any evil spiritual garments."

3. Plead the blood of Jesus over every confessed sin.

4. Rebuke in the name of Jesus, demons that have been operating against you to stir pride in your heart.

5. Now begin the prayers of thanksgiving to the Lord for His past benefits, His present care, and His future blessings for you.

6. Pray: "O Lord, hide me in the secret place of Your presence far from the great force of the pride of man, in the name of Jesus."

7. Pray: "Father God, mar the great pride of man that is set to invest me with evil spiritual garments of sorrow" (see Jer. 13:9).

8. Declare: "By the power of the Holy Spirit, I come against the great force of the foot of pride that is set against me, in the name of Jesus."

9. Declare: "Every wicked mind that is hardened in pride to hinder me from fulfilling my divine purpose, the Lord rebuke you, in the name of Jesus."

10. Declare: "In the name of Jesus, my heart shall not be lifted up in pride to my destruction."

11. Declare: "In the name of Jesus, the pride of life shall not invest me with any garment of hindrance."

12. Declare: "I say by my authority in the third heaven that the great force of the pride of man's heart shall not prevail or bring me down from my throne of glory, in the name of Jesus."

13. Declare: "By the blood of Jesus, I cut off the pride of evil men assigned to hinder my progress" (see Job 35:12).

14. Declare: "Demonic powers projecting pride into my heart to stop me from getting to my promised land, you are lying. Therefore, I command you to be paralyzed, in the name of Jesus."

15. Pray: "In the name of Jesus, the glory of God shall overshadow me and the power of pride shall be broken in my life."

16. Pray, "Thank You, Jesus, for giving me victory over the great force of pride."

✝ Prayers to Deal With the Great Force of Lust

Bear in mind during this prayer program that the body is the physical garment that covers the spirit and soul. The body can be both defiled and cleansed. When the body is defiled through unholy sex, it will attract no good thing to its owner. When it is cleansed, blessing is released.

Bible Links to Prayer Guides

And it came to pass after this, that Absalom the son of David had a fair sister, whose name was Tamar; and Amnon the son of David loved her. And Amnon was so vexed, that he fell sick for his sister Tamar; for she was a virgin; and Amnon thought it hard for him to do anything to her (2 Sam. 13:1-2).

*And, behold, there met him a woman with **the attire of an harlot**, and subtil of heart* (Prov. 7:10, emphasis added).

Lust not after her beauty in thine heart; neither let her take thee with her eyelids. For by means of a whorish woman a man is brought to a piece of bread: and the adulteress will hunt for the precious life (Prov. 6:25-26).

PRAYER FOCUS

• To deal with any appetite for unholy sex
• To destroy the spiritual harlotry garments invested by the great force of lust

PRAYER GUIDES

1. Purpose to enter this prayer program with a heart of spiritual violence to take or remove by force (see Matt. 11:12).

2. Pray: "O Lord, in the name of Jesus, forgive my sins and the sins of my ancestors that have invested me with evil spiritual garments of harlotry.

3. Plead the blood of Jesus over every confessed sin.

4. Rebuke in the name of Jesus, demons that have been operating against your life due to any of the sins you have just confessed.

5. Now begin the prayers of thanksgiving to the Lord for His past benefits, His present care, and His future blessings for you.

6. Declare: "In the name of Jesus, I put on the divine garments of righteousness to destroy the evil appetite for unholy sex."

7. Declare: "I bind and cast out from my spirit, soul, and body, demons of pornography, by the power in the blood of Jesus."

8. Declare: "With the blood of Jesus, I cut off every demonic projection of pornographic images into my mind."

9. Declare: "With the blood of Jesus, and in His name, I shield my mind from any demonic pornographic stimulation."

10. Pray: "Lord, let my mind be released from the attack of the great force of pornography, in the name of Jesus."

11. Declare: "In the name of Jesus, I command the activities of the great force of masturbation to expire in my life."

12. Declare: "Every personality dressed in spiritual garments of harlotry and assigned to seduce me into fornication, the Lord rebuke you. Depart from me, in the name of Jesus."

13. Declare: "Every personality dressed in spiritual garments of harlotry and assigned to seduce me into adultery, the Lord rebuke you! Depart from me, in the name of Jesus."

14. Declare: "By the power in the blood of Jesus, I remove the evil spiritual garments of harlotry and I put on the spiritual garments of holiness."

15. Declare: "Any demonic power propelling the great force of lust into my heart so as to clothe me with the evil spiritual garments of harlotry, be paralyzed, in the name of Jesus."

16. Pray and thank the Lord for your victory in this prayer program.

Chapter 8

Destroying Garments
of Hindrance

Garments of hindrance are invested in us through the great forces already discussed. Once we become aware of the investiture of these evil spiritual garments, we are empowered— by the blood of the Lamb and through the Holy Spirit—to remove and replace them!

✟ PRAYERS TO DEAL WITH SPIRITUAL GARMENTS OF CAPTIVITY

BIBLE LINKS TO PRAYER GUIDES

*And she shall **put the raiment of her captivity from off her**, and shall remain in thine house, and bewail her father and her mother a full month: and after that thou shalt go in unto her, and be her husband, and she shall be thy wife* (Deut. 21:13, emphasis added).

And he said unto Abram, Know of a surety that thy seed shall be a stranger in a land that is not theirs, and shall serve them; and they shall afflict them four hundred years; (Gen. 15:13).

PRAYER FOCUS

- To destroy spiritual garments of captivity
- To be invested with divine garments of liberty
- To come against the great force of oppression that changes garments from goodly to evil
- To destroy the afflicting power of the spiritual garments of captivity
- To be set free

PRAYER GUIDES

1. Purpose to enter this prayer program with a heart of spiritual violence to take or remove by force (see Matt. 11:12).

2. Pray: "O Lord, forgive my sins and the sins of my ancestors that have invested me with spiritual garments of captivity."

3. Plead the blood of Jesus over every confessed sin.

4. Rebuke in the name of Jesus, demons that have been operating against your life due to any of the sins you have just confessed.

5. Now begin the prayers of thanksgiving to the Lord for His past benefits, His present care, and His future blessings for you.

6. Declare: "Evil spiritual garments of captivity inherited from my parents, catch fire and burn to ashes, in the name of Jesus."

7. Declare: "Ancestral garments of captivity binding my people from prospering, I tear you to pieces, in the name of Jesus."

8. Declare: "Ancestral garments of captivity passed down to my generation, I tear you into pieces, in the name of Jesus."

9. Declare: "Territorial spirits investing me with spiritual garments of captivity, be paralyzed, in the name of Jesus."

10. Declare: "In the name of Jesus, I command every ancestral spirit assigned to invest me with spiritual garments of captivity to be paralyzed."

11. Declare: "In the name of Jesus, I bind any territorial spirit attempting to invest me with spiritual garments of captivity."

12. Declare: "Any territorial spirit assigned to clothe me in spiritual garments of captivity and backwardness, be paralyzed, in the name of Jesus."

13. Declare: "By the power in the blood of Jesus, I destroy the afflicting power of the spiritual garments of captivity."

14. Declare: "By my authority in the third heaven, I come against the great force of oppression that changes spiritual garments of liberty to spiritual garments of captivity."

15. Declare: "By my authority in the third heaven, I put on the spiritual garments of liberty to repel the great force of oppression."

16. Pray and thank the Lord for empowering you to overcome the hold of the spiritual garment of captivity.

✞ PRAYERS TO DEAL WITH SPIRITUAL GARMENTS OF THE GRAVE AND OF UNTIMELY DEATH

BIBLE LINKS TO PRAYER GUIDES

*And he that was dead came forth, bound hand and foot with **grave clothes**: and his face was bound about with a napkin. Jesus saith unto them, Loose him, and let him go* (John 11:44, emphasis added).

In those days was Hezekiah sick unto death. And the prophet Isaiah the son of Amoz came to him, and said unto him, Thus saith the LORD, Set thine house in order; for thou shalt die, and not live (2 Kings 20:1).

But if the wicked will turn from all his sins that he hath committed, and keep all my statutes, and do that which is lawful and right, he shall surely live, he shall not die (Ezek. 18:21).

I shall not die, but live, and declare the works of the LORD (Ps. 118:17).

PRAYER FOCUS

- To destroy evil spiritual garments of the grave and untimely death
- To be invested with divine garments of long life
- To banish the great force of sickness that invests evil spiritual garments of untimely death, by the blood of Jesus

PRAYER GUIDES

1. Purpose to enter this prayer program with a heart of spiritual violence to take or remove by force (see Matt. 11:12).

2. Pray: "O Lord, in the name of Jesus, forgive my sins and the sins of my ancestors that have invested me with evil spiritual garments of untimely death."

3. Plead the blood of Jesus over every confessed sin.

4. Rebuke in the name of Jesus, demons that have been operating against your life due to any of the sins you have just confessed.

5. Now begin the prayers of thanksgiving to the Lord for His past benefits, His present care, and His future blessings for you.

6. Declare: "Spiritual garments of untimely death passed down to my generation, be roasted by fire, in the name of Jesus."

7. Declare: "I reject any spiritual garments of untimely death prepared for me by the great force of witchcraft, in the name of Jesus."

8. Declare: "In the name of Jesus, I refuse to wear the spiritual garments of untimely death assigned to me by ancestral powers."

9. Pray: "Let the blood of Jesus swallow every sin that has invested me with the spiritual garments of untimely death; and let that blood set me free, in Jesus' name."

10. Pray: "Let the fire of the Holy Ghost burn to ashes any garment of the grave assigned to bind my glory, in the name of Jesus."

11. Pray: "Lord Jesus, You are the resurrection and the life. Take away from me the spiritual garments of the

grave and untimely death and invest me with the spiritual garments of life."

12. Pray: "Father God, command Your angels to come forth and loose me from the grave clothes binding me from moving forward, in the name of Jesus."

14. Pray: "Thank You, Jesus, for answering my prayers."

✟ PRAYERS TO DEAL WITH THE SPIRITUAL GARMENTS OF POVERTY

BIBLE LINKS TO PRAYER GUIDES

Save now, I beseech thee, O LORD: O LORD, I beseech thee, send now prosperity (Ps. 118:25).

There is that scattereth, and yet increaseth; and there is that withholdeth more than is meet, but it tendeth to poverty (Prov. 11:24).

PRAYER FOCUS

- To destroy the great force of a power of darkness that is assigned to invest spiritual garments of poverty
- To be empowered by the Holy Spirit to remove spiritual garments of poverty

PRAYER GUIDES

1. Purpose to enter this prayer program with a heart of spiritual violence to take or remove by force (see Matt. 11:12).

2. Pray: "O Lord, forgive my sins and the sins of my ancestors that have invested me with spiritual garments of poverty."

3. Plead the blood of Jesus over every confessed sin.

4. Rebuke in the name of Jesus, demons that have been operating against your life due to any of the sins you have just confessed.

5. Now begin the prayers of thanksgiving to the Lord for His past benefits, His present care, and His future blessings for you.

6. Pray: "I hold up the blood of Jesus against any great force of darkness that is assigned to clothe me with the spiritual garments of poverty, in the name of Jesus."

7. Declare: "Every satanic conspiracy that has resulted in my wearing spiritual garments of poverty, scatter, in the name of Jesus."

8. Declare: "In the name of Jesus, I reject any evil spiritual garment designed to bring shame and embarrassment to me."

9. Declare: "I reject every spiritual garment of poverty and financial failure prepared for me by the great forces of the environment in which I live, in the name of Jesus."

10. Declare: "I enter into the Lord's covenant of prosperity; therefore spiritual garments of financial failure and poverty have no hold on me, in Jesus' name."

11. Declare: "By the power of the Holy Spirit, I put on spiritual garments of prosperity, in the name of Jesus."

12. Declare: "By the power of the Holy Spirit, I recover every blessing and fortune turned away from me by spiritual garments of poverty, in the name of Jesus."

13. Pray: "O Lord, invest me now with the divine garments of prosperity that will draw back to me divine blessings and fortunes previously blocked from me by the spiritual garments of poverty, in the name of Jesus.

14. Pray and thank the Lord for giving you victory over the spiritual garments of poverty.

✞ PRAYERS TO DEAL WITH FILTHY GARMENTS INVESTED IN A MINISTER OF THE GOSPEL

When ministers are compromised by garments of hindrance, the effects upon the minister, the Church, and the Kingdom are profound. But, praise the Lord—filthy garments can be removed and replaced!

BIBLE LINKS TO PRAYER GUIDES

And he shewed me Joshua the high priest standing before the angel of the LORD, and Satan standing at his right hand to resist him. And the LORD said unto Satan, The LORD rebuke thee, O Satan; even the LORD that hath chosen Jerusalem rebuke thee: is not this a brand plucked out of the fire? Now Joshua was clothed with filthy garments, and stood before the angel (Zech. 3:1-3).

But we are all as an unclean thing, and all our righteousnesses are as filthy rags; and we all do fade as a leaf; and our iniquities, like the wind, have taken us away (Isa. 64:6).

PRAYER FOCUS

• To destroy any filthy spiritual garments designed to undermine ministers of the gospel
• To be invested with divine garments of holiness

• To come against the great force of sin that results in the wearing of filthy spiritual garments

PRAYER GUIDES

1. Purpose to enter this prayer program with a heart of spiritual violence to take or remove by force (see Matt. 11:12).

2. Pray: "O Lord, in the name of Jesus, forgive my sins and the sins of my ancestors that have invested me with filthy spiritual garments."

3. Plead the blood of Jesus over every confessed sin.

4. Rebuke in the name of Jesus, demons that have been operating against your life due to any of the sins you have just confessed.

5. Pray: "Lord Jesus, as I enter this prayer program, I thank You for the redemptive power in Your blood that redeems my life from any filthy spiritual garments."

6. Pray: "Lord Jesus, I thank You for the divine garments of salvation You made available to me through the Cross."

7. Declare: "Filthy spiritual garments assigned against my calling and ministry, catch fire and burn, in the name of Jesus."

8. Declare: "My priestly garments shall not be exchanged for filthy spiritual garments, in the name of Jesus."

9. Declare: "My priestly garments shall not be corrupted by the great force of lust, in the name of Jesus."

10. Declare: "My priestly garments shall not be changed by the force of wickedness, in the name of Jesus."

11. Declare: "My priestly garments shall not wax old, in the name of Jesus."

12. Declare: "Forces of wickedness assigned to change my priestly garments, the Lord rebuke you, in the name of Jesus."

13. Declare: "Evil assignments projected against my calling to make my priestly garments filthy, go back to your sender, in the name of Jesus."

14. Declare: "By the blood of Jesus, I overcome every demonic agenda contrived to invest me with filthy garments."

15. Declare: "In the name of Jesus, I refuse to wear the filthy garments prepared for me by contrary powers whose purpose is the termination of my calling."

16. Pray: "Thank You, Jesus, for giving me victory over the power of filthy spiritual garments."

Chapter 9

Entering Investiture With Divine Garments

To remove ungodly spiritual garments is the first part of a two-fold process. The second part is to replace those garments with the divine garments that signify the righteousness of God.

The following prayers are tailored for this purpose. As always, seek the guidance and wisdom of the Holy Spirit as you proceed. He will reveal more to you than any book can contain.

✟ Prayers That Invest Garments of Salvation

The foundation garments of salvation are the spiritual vestments unbelievers put on at conversion. These garments separate those who are in Christ from those who are not yet redeemed with His blood.

Bible Links to Prayer Guides

*I will greatly rejoice in the Lord, my soul shall be joyful in my God; for he hath **clothed me with the garments of salvation**, he hath covered me with the robe of righteousness, as a bridegroom decketh himself with ornaments, and* *as a bride adorneth herself with her jewels* (Isa. 61:10, emphasis added).

Now therefore arise, O LORD God, into thy resting place, thou, and the ark of thy strength: let thy priests, O LORD God, be clothed with salvation, and let thy saints rejoice in goodness (2 Chron. 6:41).

I will also clothe her priests with salvation: and her saints shall shout aloud for joy (Ps. 132:16).

For the LORD taketh pleasure in his people: he will beautify the meek with salvation (Ps. 149:4).

PRAYER FOCUS

- For the unsaved to be invested with garments of salvation, the foundation of all goodly garments
- To overcome any force set against the garments of salvation

PRAYER GUIDES

1. Purpose to enter this prayer program with a heart of genuine repentance.

2. Pray: "O Lord, in the name of Jesus, forgive my sins and any sins of my ancestors that have invested me with any garment of hindrance."

3. Plead the blood of Jesus over every confessed sin.

4. Rebuke in the name of Jesus, demons that have been operating against your life due to any of the sins you have just confessed.

5. Pray: "Lord Jesus, as I enter this prayer program, I thank You for the redemptive power in Your blood that has made a way for me to be invested with the garments of salvation."

6. Pray: "O Lord, in the name of Jesus, destroy any bad habits that are set against my garments of salvation."

7. Declare: "Evil assignments programmed to hinder my wearing of the garments of salvation, expire to the glory of God, in the name of Jesus."

8. Declare: "Witchcraft projections sent to remove my garments of salvation, be cut off with the blood of Jesus."

9. Pray: "Lord, adorn me with the garments of salvation that I may rejoice in it" (see Ps. 9:14).

10. Pray: "Father God, empower me to wear the garments of salvation that I may be set up on high, in the name of Jesus" (see Ps. 69:29).

11. Pray: "Father God, invest me with the garments of salvation that I may be empowered against the forces of the waster, in the name of Jesus."

12. Pray: "O, Ancient of Days, scatter any activity of ancestral spirits that stands contrary to my investiture with the garments of salvation, in the name of Jesus."

13. Pray: "Let the victorious power of the Cross invest me now with the garments of salvation, in the name of Jesus."

14. Pray: "Thank You, Jesus, for answering my prayers."

✟ Prayers That Invest With the Divine Garments of Praise

It is important to remember that the spirit of heaviness is a great force that invests spiritual garments of sorrow. The garment of praise overcomes this great force.

Bible Links to Prayer Guides

*To appoint unto them that mourn in Zion, to give unto them beauty for ashes, the oil of joy for mourning, **the garment of praise for the spirit of heaviness;** that they might be called trees of righteousness, the planting of the LORD, that he might be glorified* (Isa. 61:3, emphasis added).

The living, the living, he shall praise thee, as I do this day: the father to the children shall make known thy truth (Isa. 38:19).

Prayer Focus

• To be permanently invested with the divine garments of praise to counter the onslaught of the great force of heaviness assigned by the adversary of our souls

Prayer Guides

1. Purpose to enter this prayer program with a heart of genuine repentance.

2. Pray: "O Lord, forgive my sins and the sins of my ancestors that have invested me with any garment of hindrance, in the name of Jesus."

3. Plead the blood of Jesus over every confessed sin.

4. Rebuke in the name of Jesus, demons that have been operating against your life due to any of the sins you have just confessed.

5. Pray: "Lord Jesus, as I enter this prayer program, I thank You for the redemptive power in Your blood that has made a way for me to be invested with divine garments of praise."

6. Pray: "Lord Jesus, I thank You for the spiritual garments of salvation You made available to me through the Cross."

7. Pray: "O Lord, in the name of Jesus, clothe me with the garments of praise to ward off the attack of the spirit of heaviness."

8. Declare: "In the name of Jesus, the great force of the spirit of heaviness shall not strip away my divine garments of praise."

9. Declare: "In the name of Jesus, the great forces of lamentation and crying shall not strip away my divine garments of praise."

10. Pray: "Lord Jesus, invest me now with the divine garments of praise as you did for King David."

11. Declare: "Demonic powers assigned to remove my divine garments of praise, the Lord rebuke you, in the name of Jesus."

12. Declare: "In the name of Jesus, I put on the divine garments of praise to overcome demonic afflictions assigned to take away my joy."

13. Declare: "In the name of Jesus, I put on the divine garments of praise to overcome demonic oppressions assigned to burden my spirit."

14. Declare: "By the power of the Holy Spirit I am invested now with the divine garments of praise to dismantle the habitation of weariness in my life, in the name of Jesus."

15. Declare: "By the power of the Holy Spirit, I am invested with the divine garments of praise to repel and send back the arrows of sorrow thrust at me by satanic agents, in the name of Jesus."

16. Pray: "Thank You, Jesus, for answering my prayers."

✝ PRAYERS THAT INVEST DIVINE WHITE AND SHINING GARMENTS

BIBLE LINKS TO PRAYER GUIDES

Let thy garments be always white; and let thy head lack no ointment (Eccles. 9:8).

And after six days Jesus taketh Peter, James, and John his brother, and bringeth them up into an high mountain apart, and was transfigured before them: and his face did shine as the sun, and his raiment was white as the light (Matt. 17:1-2).

And his raiment became shining, exceeding white as snow; so as no fuller on earth can white them (Mark 9:3).

Thou hast a few names even in Sardis which have not defiled their garments; and they shall walk with me in white: for they are worthy (Rev. 3:4).

I beheld till the thrones were cast down, and the Ancient of days did sit, whose garment was white as snow, and the hair of his head like the pure wool: his throne was like the fiery flame, and his wheels as burning fire (Dan. 7:9).

And no marvel; for Satan himself is transformed into an angel of light (2 Cor. 11:14).

PRAYER FOCUS

• To be invested with the divine white and shining garments, through the great forces of holiness and prayer

PRAYER GUIDES

1. Purpose to enter this prayer program with a heart of genuine repentance.

2. Pray: "O Lord, in the name of Jesus, forgive my sins and the sins of my ancestors that have invested me with any garment of hindrance."

3. Plead the blood of Jesus over every confessed sin.

4. Rebuke in the name of Jesus, demons that have been operating against your life due to any of the sins you have just confessed.

5. Pray: "Lord Jesus, as I enter this prayer program, I thank You for the redemptive power in Your blood that has made a way for me to be invested with divine white and shining garments."

6. Pray: "Lord Jesus, I thank You for the garments of salvation You made available to me through the Cross."

7. Declare: "O great force of my father's house assigned to hinder my investiture with divine white and shining garments, be paralyzed by the thunder of God, in the name of Jesus."

8. Declare: "O great forces of my environment (territorial spirits), you shall not succeed in soiling my divine white garments, in the name of Jesus."

9. Declare: "Demonic powers assigned to program corruption against my divine white garments, I rebuke you in the name of Jesus."

10. Declare: "Demonic powers assigned to program errors into my thinking in order to defile my divine white garments, you are lying spirits and you shall fail woefully, in the name of Jesus."

11. Declare: "Satanic agents assigned to stain my spiritual white garments, the Lord Jesus rebuke you."

12. Declare: "My divine shining garments shall not be soiled by the careless words of my mouth, in Jesus' name."

13. Pray: "O Lord, let my spiritual garments be always white, in the name of Jesus."

14. Declare: "My divine white garments shall not be soiled by the cares of this world, in the name of Jesus."

15. Pray: "O Lord, empower me by Your Holy Spirit to walk with You in white garments, in the name of Jesus."

16. Pray: "O Lord, empower me to keep a pure heart, so that my garments might remain white and shining always, in the name of Jesus."

17. "Thank You, Jesus, for giving me victory in this prayer program."

✟ PRAYERS THAT INVEST WITH DIVINE BEAUTIFUL GARMENTS

BIBLE LINKS TO PRAYER GUIDES

Awake, awake; put on thy strength, O Zion; put on thy beautiful garments, O Jerusalem, the holy city: for henceforth there shall no more come into thee the uncircumcised and the unclean (Isa. 52:1).

Now Israel loved Joseph more than all his children, because he was the son of his old age: and he made him a coat of many colours (Gen. 37:3).

And thou shalt make holy garments for Aaron thy brother for glory and for beauty (Exod. 28:2).

PRAYER FOCUS

• To be clothed in divine beautiful garments that repel contrary spirits
• To stop the great forces of unbelief and idolatry from defiling my divine beautiful garments

PRAYER GUIDES

1. Purpose to enter this prayer program with a heart of genuine repentance.

2. O Lord, forgive my sins and the sins of my ancestors that have invested me with a spiritual garment of hindrance, in the name of Jesus.

3. Plead the blood of Jesus upon every confessed sin.

4. Rebuke in the name of Jesus, demons that have been operating against your life due to any of the sins you have just confessed.

5. Pray: "Lord Jesus, as I enter this prayer program, I thank You for the redemptive power in Your blood that has made a way for me to be invested with divine beautiful garments."

6. Pray: "Lord Jesus, I thank You for the foundation garments of salvation You made available to me through the Cross."

7. Pray: "Father God, invest me with the divine beautiful garments that will ward off polluting spirits, in the name of Jesus."

8. Declare: "My divine beautiful garments shall not be damaged by the great force of envious friends, in the name of Jesus."

9. Pray: "Lord Jesus, assign to me angels that will invest me with my own divine beautiful garments, in the name of Jesus" (see Zech. 3:5).

10. Declare: "Powers assigned to change my divine beautiful garments to contrary garments, you shall not succeed, in the name of Jesus."

11. Pray: "Let the good hand of the Lord be upon me and invest me now with divine beautiful garments

for honor and great accomplishments, in the name of Jesus" (see Ezra 7:9).

12. Pray: "O Lord, invest me with the beautiful divine garments that will empower my life with dominion prosperity (prosperity that is unaffected by economic downturns), in the name of Jesus."

13. Pray: "O Lord, invest me with the divine beautiful garments that will broadcast Your name in my life and bring You glory, in the name of Jesus."

14. Declare: "By the Word of the Lord, my divine beautiful garments shall remain with me and shall not be cast off, in the name of Jesus."

15. Pray: "Thank You, Jesus, for answering my prayers."

✝ PRAYERS THAT INVEST HOLY GARMENTS

Often, the redeemed children of God are hindered in their efforts to operate as believers because of demonic covenants made by their ancestors through idol worship and other ungodly practices (see Ps. 74:20 and Lev. 26:45).

Demonic powers always strive to enforce these covenants. They will succeed in doing so *unless* the believer becomes aware of the *specific* covenant and revokes it spiritually. This means appropriating the blood of Jesus to neutralize the unholy "contract."

BIBLE LINKS TO PRAYER GUIDES

And thou shalt make holy garments for Aaron thy brother for glory and for beauty (Exod. 28:2).

And these are the garments which they shall make; a breastplate, and an ephod, and a robe, and a broidered coat, a miter, and a girdle: and they shall make holy gar-

ments for Aaron thy brother, and his sons, that he may minister unto me in the priest's office (Exod. 28:4).

And the holy garments of Aaron shall be his sons' after him, to be anointed therein, and to be consecrated in them (Exod. 29:29).

PRAYER FOCUS

• To be invested with holy garments that will bring glory and beauty
• To deal with the great force of ancestral spirits that denies investiture with the holy garments

PRAYER GUIDES

1. Purpose to enter this prayer program with a heart of genuine repentance.

2. Pray: "O Lord, in the name of Jesus, forgive my sins and the sins of my ancestors that have invested me with a garment of hindrance, in the name of Jesus."

3. Plead the blood of Jesus over every confessed sin.

4. Rebuke in the name of Jesus, demons that have been operating against your life due to any of the sins you have just confessed.

5. Pray: "Lord Jesus, as I enter this prayer program, I thank You for the redemptive power in Your blood that has made a way for me to be invested with holy garments."

6. Pray: "Lord Jesus, I thank You for the garments of salvation You made available to me through the Cross."

7. Pray: "O God, who invested Aaron and his generations with the holy garments, arise in Your overriding power and invest me now with my holy garments, in the name of Jesus."

8. Pray: "O Lord, send Your angels to come and invest me now with my own holy garments for ministerial accomplishment, in the name of Jesus."

9. Pray: "Anointing that invests God's people with holy garments, come upon me now, in the name of Jesus" (see Zech. 3:5).

10. Pray: "O Lord, invest me now with holy garments for honor and beauty, to your glory, in the name of Jesus."

11. Pray: "O Lord, invest me with the holy garments that will empower me to minister unto You in the priest's office forever, in the name of Jesus."

12. Declare: "Any demonic power assigned to hinder me from wearing holy garments, be paralyzed, in the name of Jesus."

13. Declare: "Ancestral powers resisting my investiture with holy garments, the Lord rebuke you, in the name of Jesus."

14. Declare: "Every power assigned to stain my holy garments, the Lord rebuke you, in the name of Jesus."

15. Declare: "In the name of Jesus, my holy garments shall not be spotted by the works of the flesh" (see Jude 23).

16. Declare: "In the name of Jesus, my holy garments shall not be changed by the great force of the wasters, in the name of Jesus" (see Isa. 54:16).

17. "Thank You, Jesus, for giving me victory in this prayer program."

✞ TARGETED PRAYERS TO CALL FORTH DIVINE GARMENTS PARTS A, B, AND C
(SEE BELOW)

BIBLE LINKS TO PRAYER GUIDES

Again he said unto me, Prophesy upon these bones, and say unto them, O ye dry bones, hear the word of the LORD. Thus saith the Lord GOD unto these bones; Behold, I will cause breath to enter into you, and ye shall live: (Ezek. 37:4-5).

Moreover the word of the LORD came unto me, saying, Son of man, set thy face toward the south, and drop thy word toward the south, and prophesy against the forest of the south field; and say to the forest of the south, Hear the word of the LORD; Thus saith the Lord GOD; Behold, I will kindle a fire in thee, and it shall devour every green tree in thee, and every dry tree: the flaming flame shall not be quenched, and all faces from the south to the north shall be burned therein (Ezek. 20:45-47).

A. TARGETED PRAYERS TO INVEST DIVINE GARMENTS

PRAYER FOCUS

• To speak the words of the Lord so as to be invested with the divine garments that bring promotion, success, prosperity, and fulfillment

• To engage divine great forces to counter the activities of the evil great forces investing garments of hindrance

PRAYER GUIDES

1. Pray: "O God who created the heavens and the earth, arise, and enforce my investiture with the spiritual garments that will move me forward today, in the name of Jesus."

2. Pray: "Ancient of Days, come in Your unchanging white garment and invest me with Your garments that never wax old, in the name of Jesus" (see Dan. 7:9).

3. Pray: "Let the Holy Spirit clothe me in spiritual garments that will make me increase in favor with God and man, in the name of Jesus" (see Luke 2:52).

4. Declare: "I put off the spiritual garments of 'almost there' and I put on the spiritual garments of 'arriving there' by the empowerment of the Holy Spirit, in Jesus' name."

5. Pray: "Let the glory of the Lord overshadow and empower my spiritual garments to stay white and beautiful, in the name of Jesus."

6. Declare: "All the days of my life, my spiritual garments shall be white, shining, and beautiful, in the name of Jesus."

7. Declare: "I receive the garments of fire for ministerial accomplishment, in the name of Jesus."

8. Pray: "Father God, as You removed the spiritual garments of prison from Joseph, remove them from me,

and invest me with the fine linen garments of liberty, in the name of Jesus" (see Gen. 41:42).

9. Pray: "O Lord, as you did for Jabez, change my spiritual garments of sorrow to spiritual garments of honor, in the name of Jesus" (see 1 Chron. 4:9).

10. Pray: "O Lord, invest me with spiritual garments that will change my story to glory, in Jesus' name."

11. Pray: "O Lord, invest me with the divine garments that will make the impossible possible in my life, in the name of Jesus."

B. TARGETED PRAYERS TO DIVEST DEMONIC SPIRITUAL GARMENTS

PRAYER FOCUS

• To speak the words of the Lord to remove any garment of hindrance designed for the purpose of killing, destroying, and stealing
• To rebuke, in the name of Jesus, the great forces assigned to invest garments of hindrance

PRAYER GUIDES

1. Pray: "O God of mercy and grace, who removed the garment of hindrance invested on Joshua the high priest, remove any spiritual garment of hindrance invested in me by ancestral spirits, in the name of Jesus."

2. Pray: "O God of mercy and grace, who removed the garment of hindrance invested on Joshua the high priest, remove today any spiritual garments of reproach and affliction (be specific if you are aware of

specific areas that apply to your life) invested in me by powers of witchcraft, in the name of Jesus."

3. Pray: "Father God, come as Jehovah and release me from the hold and power of any inherited evil spiritual garments that bring me failure at the edge of breakthrough, in the name of Jesus."

4. Declare: "Evil spiritual garment that has put me in the wilderness of life, be roasted in the fire of God, in the name of Jesus."

5. Declare: "I reject any spiritual garment of hindrance sewn by the great force of the wickedness of my past generations, in the name of Jesus."

6. Pray: "Let the sacrificial blood of Jesus nullify the evil effects of every demonic garment I have ever unconsciously worn, in the name of Jesus."

7. Declare: "Any demonic power that wants to bewitch my destiny through the investiture of a spiritual garment of hindrance, be struck and paralyzed now, by the lightning of God, in Jesus' name."

8. Pray: "Father God, as You removed the spiritual garments of reproach from Hannah, remove them from me, so that my mouth would be enlarged over my enemies, in the name of Jesus" (see 1 Sam. 2:1).

9. Pray: "Father God, as You removed the spiritual garments of sorrow from Hannah, remove them from me, that my heart might rejoice in You, in the name of Jesus" (see 1 Sam. 2:1).

10. Pray: "Father God, as You ended the activities of the great force of bitterness in the life of Hannah, let such

bitterness of soul end in my life today, that I might rejoice in your salvation, in the name of Jesus " (see 1 Sam. 1:10; 2:1).

11. Pray: "Father God, as You removed contrary garments from Joseph, remove from me those garments put on me by the household enemies of my glorious destiny, in the name of Jesus."

12. Declare: "Every great force that seeks to invest contrary spiritual garments in me, be paralyzed, in the name of Jesus."

13. Pray: "Father God, come as Jehovah and release me from the hold of evil spiritual garments of captivity, in the name of Jesus."

C. TARGETED PRAYERS AGAINST DEMONIC SPIRITUAL GARMENTS

PRAYER FOCUS

• To neutralize the evil effect of specific garments of hindrance
• To be released from the hold of specific garments of hindrance

PRAYER GUIDES

1. Pray: "Let the blood of Jesus stagnate the activities of the great force of wicked associates conspiring to invest me with a garment of hindrance."

2. Declare: "Evil spiritual garments of untimely death demonically prepared for me by agents of witchcraft, catch fire and burn to ashes, in the name of Jesus."

3. Pray: "O Lord, destroy any evil spiritual garment prepared by envious household enemies (witchcraft or occult practiced in the family) to bring shame and dishonor to me, in the name of Jesus."

4. Declare: "Evil spiritual garments demonically removed from someone else and assigned to be transferred to me by satanic agents, catch fire and burn to ashes, in the name of Jesus."

5. Declare: "Every demonic power attempting to clothe me in contrary spiritual garments, be paralyzed, in the name of Jesus."

6. Declare: "I challenge with Holy Ghost fire any contrary garment put upon my children by agents of darkness, and I command them to burn to ashes, in the name of Jesus."

7. Declare: "Any garment of hindrance assigned to bring rebellion and disobedience into the lives of my children, the Lord rebuke you. Become powerless, in the name of Jesus."

8. Declare: "Every spiritual garment designed by dark powers to keep my life moving in a circle, catch fire and burn to ashes, in the name of Jesus."

9. Declare: "Spiritual garments of captivity assigned to establish bitterness in my life, catch fire and burn to ashes, in the name of Jesus."

10. Declare: "Any evil spiritual garment invested in me to keep me perpetually in debt, be removed by the power of the Holy Spirit and let me begin to live in abundance, in the name of Jesus."

11. Declare: "Any power who has tried to hinder my progress by clothing me in any evil spiritual garments, the Lord rebuke you, in the name of Jesus."

12. Declare: "Any demonic power projecting the great force of lust into my heart in order to invest me with an evil spiritual garment, I cut off your projection with the blood of Jesus."

13. Declare: "Any demonic power that has tried to draw me into error by investing me with garments of deceit, your endeavor shall fail, in the name of Jesus."

14. Declare: "Powers that want me to wear sackcloth as a garment, be paralyzed, in the name of Jesus" (see Ps. 69:11).

15. Pray: "O Lord, in the name of Jesus, deal with those who put on the garments of wickedness to oppress me."

16. Declare: "Any garment of hindrance assigned to bring disfavor in my life, be torn to pieces, in the name of Jesus."

17. Declare: "Any garment of hindrance designed for me in order to stagnate my progress, be destroyed in the fire of God."

18. Declare: "I revoke every restriction imposed upon my life and destiny by any evil spiritual garment, in the name of Jesus."

19. Declare: "Father God, come as the Ancient of Days and judge the demonic powers assigned to invest me with any evil spiritual garments, in the name of Jesus" (see Dan. 7:22).

20. Declare: "Any garment of hindrance assigned to bring marital failure in my life, be torn to pieces, in the name of Jesus."

21. Declare: "Any garment of hindrance fabricated by any demonic great force to bring financial failure in my life, catch fire and burn to ashes, in the name of Jesus."

Conclusion

"Dressed" for Success

Yes, how you dress matters—in the natural realm and, more importantly, in the spiritual realm!

Although demonic entities seek to clothe God's people in garments of hindrance, we are not subject to the wardrobe suggestions they make. Because of the shed blood of Jesus Christ, we are empowered to overcome the enemy's designs and live successfully.

What does that mean? It means that, no matter how you may have been hindered in the past, you are *still* called to experience the fulfillment of your God-ordained destiny in all areas of life. As His child, you were created to manifest the fullness of salvation and demonstrate the love, mercy, and power of God to others.

By the grace of God, you shall do just that! You are armed with knowledge and understanding. You know how to identify garments of hindrance and you know how to remove them—and, because you are His, you know how to replace "filthy" garments of darkness with divine garments sewn for you by the Almighty!

I encourage you to return to this book and these prayers often. Now that you have discovered and addressed your spiritual "wardrobe," you will want to maintain diligently it over your lifetime.

My prayer is that you would remain dressed for success always...

The eyes of your understanding being enlightened; that ye may know what is the hope of his calling, and what the riches of the glory of his inheritance in the saints, and what is the exceeding greatness of his power to usward who believe, according to the working of his mighty power, which he wrought in Christ, when he raised him from the dead, and set him at his own right hand in the heavenly places, far above all principality, and power, and might, and dominion, and every name that is named, not only in this world, but also in that which is to come: and hath put all things under his feet, and gave him to be the head over all things to the church, which is his body, the fulness of him that filleth all in all (Eph. 1:18-23).

To God be the glory, forever!

LaVergne, TN USA
04 November 2010
203542LV00002B/2/P